MAKING YOUR LIFE A SUCCESS

Michael Marnu

authorHOUSE®

AuthorHouse™ UK Ltd.
500 Avebury Boulevard
Central Milton Keynes, MK9 2BE
www.authorhouse.co.uk
Phone: 08001974150

First published by AuthorHouse 2/15/2011

ISBN: 978-1-4567-7239-0

CONTENTS

"This is an accessible book for Christians of all traditions and for thoughtful non- Christians. It considers all aspects of living a positive and fulfilled life in a clear progression of thought, using encouragement and clear instruction".

Christina Thomas – Editorial Management and Training Services. Advanced Member, Society for Editors and Proofreaders

PREFACE

Sometimes, let's be honest, life can be as much fun and as sour as scratching your eyeballs with a fork. Of course, some have a worse life than others. We all can think of a list of unenviable lives. Obviously life may never get that bad for us, to know what it is to live in a world of uncertainty and confusion, to plod through an existence of considerable pain but with little gain in real terms. Can you hide a city that is set on top of a hill, its light at night seen for miles? That is exactly what life is about. It can be compared to many real-life issues:

- Life is a journey
- Life is like a roller coaster
- Life is full of test
- Life is a race
- Life is a mixed blessing.

No matter the pressures or challenges that we face, we must refuse to give up. We must run straight to life with purpose in every step remembering always that 'there is surely a future of hope [for us], and [our] hope will not be cut off.' (Proverbs 23:18).

In this book, I will share with you wisdom, guidance and strength which revolve around philosophies, beliefs, values and character traits that have proven to be the most sustaining and valuable in life. In a generation of more questions, pain, anxiety and confusion, it is important to come to a place where you will be inspired, challenged and supported as you take the steps of a champion. This book will restore you to live the abundant life.

1

THE PARADOX OF LIFE

Anansekrom is a very popular Ghanaian family get-together that takes place every summer in a park. As I drove my daughter and niece to Offset, near Lakeside for the event, I became stuck on the M25. For no good reason the M25 was at a snarled-up standstill. It had taken me over an agonising two hours to travel just a hundred yards. In the words of Jeff Lucas, even snails were overtaking me. I did not need a prophet to convince me that it would take over a year to travel the 30 minutes' journey as calculated by the navigator. More than twenty times, I turned the ignition key and switched the engine off to save fuel. I drummed my fingers impatiently on the steering wheels, fiddled with the sound system, took a brief nap, looked bored and fed up with the tortuous traffic. I wasn't going anywhere soon.

I began to compare the situation to circumstances of life. My life is stranded in traffic. I clearly love to move forward, to feel as if I am making some progress, that I am living with authentic purpose. But the reality is different. I do steer through the years but on a joyless joyride that seems to get me nowhere. I would be glad if I could navigate through it all without too many accidents or jams. But the journey begs the question 'what is the point?' Why am I living with frustration, emptiness, despair, hopelessness, disgust, apathy or anger? What is the point of going on day after day in the same meaningless way? How can I find a sense of purpose to go on? Is life really worth living?

Then it occurred to me, 'Twelve young men committing suicide every week in the United Kingdom. The male suicide rate between the ages of 15 and 24 has soared by 70 percent since 1976 to overtake the number killed in road accidents. Young men are twice as likely to suffer depression as their predecessors a decade ago. Two out of three on the brink of killing themselves feel they have no one to turn to, according to a study by Oxford University. Every human being wants success. Everybody wants the best life can deliver. However, not many people are making it. The world at present is in a state of chaos. To many, the politicians, world economy, materialism and religion have all failed them. Everyone is looking for a solution to life's problems.

Then I realised that, in a sense, the answers to these questions are in my hands. There is a message of life. It never lowers its standards or modifies its conditions to make events readily acceptable. One may change or be changed by its terms. If a person wants life on their own terms, they may end up being sorrowful. The cycle of life has mixed blessings, and each of them has a possibility of occurring. It is quite disheartening to realise that life is strewn with the wreckage of derelict half built towers – the ruins of those who began to build and were unable to finish, Maybe I am too psychologically immature to lead my own life. Maybe I have entered the cycle of life without first pausing to reflect on the cost of doing so. Life is justified because I am a mediocre achiever and stopping at failure. Instantly my face brightened when a parable of Jesus Christ dropped into me 'Which of you, desiring to build a tower, does not first sit down and count the cost whether he has enough to complete it. Otherwise, when he has laid a foundation, and is not able to finish, all who see it begin to mock him saying, 'this man began to build, and was not able to finish'.'

In truth, I have discovered that life is not a mere passive acquiescence in a series of events. I may go through circumstances but this does not make me a winner. I have to make a positive response to life by committing myself unreservedly to it. No one can deny the fact that life includes an offer as well as a demand; opportunities as well as risks; joy as well as misery. If life offers us victories, it also demands our hard work. Life gives no encouragement whatsoever to thoughtless applicants for success. Life brings no pressure to bear on any enquirer. It 'sends irresponsible enthusiasts away empty-handed'.

The Paradox of life
Sometimes, let's be honest, life can be as much fun and as sour as scratching your eyeballs with a fork. Of course, some have a worse life than others. We all can think of a list of unenviable lives. Obviously life may never get that bad for us, to know what it is to live in a world of uncertainty and confusion, to plod through an existence of considerable pain but with little gain in real terms. Can you hide a city that is set on top of a hill, its light at night seen for miles? That is exactly what life is about. It can be compared to many real-life issues:

- Life is like a journey
- Life is like a roller coaster
- Life is full of test
- Life is like a race
- Life is a mixed blessing

Life is a journey; know where you are going
Over a century ago, David Livingstone travelled 11,000 miles on foot through uncharted jungles. Racked by disease, attacked by wild animals,

menaced by hostile tribes, even robbed by his own partners, he marched on with his Bible. He preached the Gospel and fought slavery until he won the heart of a nation and planted the seeds of emancipation in both Britain and America. On 1 May 1873, he was found dead on his knees in a dilapidated hut, in an obscure African village, all because he had a dream.

There are hundreds of circumstances, values and emotions that can drive our lives. The five most common ones are guilt, resentment and anger, fear, materialism and the need for approval. Living by purpose is the only way to really live: everything else is only existence. Without a purpose, life is like a motion without meaning, activity without direction, an event without reason. Life is trivial, petty and pointless without a purpose. In truth, living a purpose-driven life gives meaning, simplifies, motivates, prepares and focuses our lives.

Nothing much happens without a vision. When you've no personal goal that you are interested in, which means something to you, you are bound to go around in circles, feel lost and disillusioned. Life itself may seem aimless and purposeless. Can you imagine a politician without an election manifesto, or military personnel without a lay-down campaign strategy? Any attempt to achieve a goal in life without this recipe is like starting fire with water. It won't work.

Consider this: 'We see the unacceptable: do we not care? We see what is: do we not see what could be? Things could be different. We need a vision of purpose.' Vision begins with indignation over the status quo, and it grows into the earnest quest for an alternative. There is a serious dearth of visionaries and dreamers. These are the people who believe that it is possible to build a better world. They are the people who feel a responsibility for life and wish to give true meaning to their lives and to the lives of all people. They are the pathfinders of society.

Every one has a seed of purpose in them. The seed that is latent determines our future and the framework of our lives. We have a responsibility to seek and water it until it blossoms. There are many good things we can do with our lives. Write down your vision as God directed in Habakkuk 2:2.

No matter what the pressures or challenges we face, we must refuse to give up. We must run straight to life with purpose in every step remembering always that 'there is surely a future of hope [for us], and [our] hope will not be cut off.' (Proverbs 23:18) In the face of trials we must always remember that: 'Living on purpose is the path to peace.' The man without a purpose is like a ship without a rudder. He is a waif, a nothing, a no man.

Jesus Christ is a reminder that vision leads to venture, and history is on the side of venturesome faith. Losers are characterised by having few clearly stated goals other than self-pity, worries and frustration. 'There is a future hope [for us] and [our] hope will not be cut off.' (Proverbs 24:14)

Life can be a roller-coaster ... enjoy the ride
Sordid details of the sex life of Lincoln were smeared across every paper. Lincoln had been destroyed. His marriage and political career were at stake. Many people anticipated his resignation as President of the Conquerland. He proved them wrong. He reacted positively to his circumstances.

To recap: life includes an offer as well as a demand; opportunities as well as problems; joy as well as misery. If life offers you victories, it demands your hard work. The message of life is quite simple and plain. It has mixed blessings. At any time in life, anything can happen.

Many people assume troubled times are for people who have offended God. This is not true. As we march across the decades of time, we are going to meet a lot of unpleasant situations. Jesus knew we would encounter problems in this world. God does not mind trials or problems coming our way. With God as our friend, every situation will be a growing experience. (Romans 8:28) The good news is that no matter what problems we face or the strength of our enemies we have already overcome them. Jesus has overcome the world and given us the victory. Moreover, God always has a victory plan for His children. We must thrive to track the victory plan made available to us – the Holy Spirit, the Blood and name of Jesus, the Word and promises of God and our Power of Attorney to turn the minuses into pluses.

We must put on the whole armour of God and apply God-given weapons of attack and strategy appropriately. We must build upon our strengths and reduce our weaknesses by remaining in Jesus Christ. Remember always that 'For everyone born of God overcomes the world, even our faith.' (1 John 5:4)

Life is full of tests ... pass the test

In our daily lives, there have been times when we face problems. Problems come at an undetermined time. Life on earth, writes Rick Warren, is a test. We are always being tested. Our responses to people, problems, success, conflict, illness and disappointments may be tested. We may be tested by major changes, delayed promises, impossible problems, unanswered prayers, undeserved criticism and even senseless tragedies. Consider the problems as a test of your life that allows you to demonstrate the quality of your faith. The test of life would help you to develop other qualities such as humility, character and maturity.

No one is protected or sheltered from life's ups and downs. Read the biographies and autobiographies of successful people and you will discover that each of these people has encountered opposition, discouragement, setbacks and personal misfortune.

See trials as challenges and as opportunities for the glory of God to be revealed in your life. No matter how difficult the situation is, encourage yourself in the Lord. Never allow discouragement to get hold of you. 'For our light affliction, which is but for a moment, worked for us a far more exceeding and eternal weight of glory.' (2 Corinthians 4:17)

Life is like a race ... run for the crown

Colonel Sanders of Kentucky Fried Chicken fame started his worldwide enterprise after he had retired from the railroad. He drove thousands of miles marketing his chicken recipe to restaurants all over the southern states of the USA. He was rejected by nearly 500 places before he hit the jackpot. On several occasions, he slept in his car because he could not afford a motel room. Today there are thousands of Kentucky Fried Chicken franchises in hundreds of countries all over the world. Can you guess what raised Colonel to heights? It was his race for the crown.

Four things are essential in order to be a champion in a given sport:

- dedication to succeed no matter what the cost;
- passion for the game;
- single-minded determination to accomplish the task at hand; and
- willingness to train incessantly.

Life offers the opportunity for people to be winners. The winner, as in any sport, receives a prize. Those who faithfully fight the good fight are rewarded. They become fulfilled. We must have a clearly defined goal in life. Like an athlete preparing for a race or a boxer a boxing match, we must discipline ourselves to maintain the strenuous consistent practice needed for success. If we ignore or treat lightly our responsibilities, we become victims of life.

It sounds ridiculous, until you realise that life is war. As we choose a course of action in order to satisfy our insatiable desires, most of these decisions relate to future outcomes and therefore involve considerations relating to uncertainty. Considering the fact that decisions are made under conditions of uncertainty and are influenced by the likelihood of future events, there is a probability that anything – good, bad, victory, setback, failure – can happen. Every situation – times of need, plenty, poverty or riches – has the chance to happen.

It was time to re-start the car and embark on another epic crawl on the M25. And as I inched my way forward, I realised again that a major roadblock is up ahead of us all, whoever we are –rich or poor young or old, male or female, able or disabled. Such is life. Living without its true perspective means decades of dullness.

2

UNDERSTANDING TROUBLES IN LIFE

Nearly 400 people were killed in an all-night assault in Sri Lanka's war zone forcing thousands to flee for makeshift shelters. Probably many more than the 378 reported were killed in the violence but they were buried where they fell, wrote a tabloid newspaper in May 2009.

If God is all-powerful, loving, wise and just, why is His world, the world He created, in a total mess? Far be it from God to do evil, from the Almighty to do wrong. (Job 34:10) God does not sin and is never unjust. There may be elements of truth in our speeches but, unfortunately, the nuggets of truth are buried under layers of false assumptions and conclusions. The truth is that our world, which reflects an invisible spirit world, is laying in the power and influence of the wicked one, Satan. (1 John 5:19) Satan is hateful, deceptive and is misleading the entire inhabited world (Revelation 12:9) into hatred, deceit and cruelty.

We are also responsible for the misery. Our greediness, selfishness and ignorance (imperfect and sinful) lead us to struggle for dominance, resulting in wars, oppression and suffering (Ecclesiastes 4:1; Ecclesiastes 8:9). Moreover, some people may suffer because they happen to be at the wrong place at the wrong time. (Ecclesiastes 9:11)

Experiencing the wilderness

Janet, the daughter of a mass murderer, was pulled from a river after an apparent suicide bid. She appeared to have thrown herself into the icy waters days after re-visiting the so called 'House of Horror'. It was there that she was sexually abused by her father and her step-mother. Her half-sister was among nine victims buried in hidden graves. She said after her visit: 'I don't know if I can take it anymore. I can still see all their faces and I can still see where they were lying. I've cried so much I don't think I have any more tears left. People say I'm lucky to have survived – but I wish I had died.' Janet's situation seems to have broken her.

In our daily lives, there are times when we face challenges that are beyond our ability. We come to the 'blackest depression of our lives'. It is more than we can take. The troubles may be beyond our ability. The situation may choke us. We lose control and appear to have no ability whatsoever. We then start to doubt our capacity. The situation can either make or break us. If we react improperly to the situation, the situation can rob us of the skills, control and ability that we can ordinarily call upon.

Some people, however, perform better under adverse circumstances. The situation itself seems to give them more strength, power and ability than they ordinarily possess. Sordid details of the sex life of Mercy and Martin were smeared across every paper. President Martin seemed destroyed. His marriage and political career were at stake. He amazed the world when he put on a public display of affection in the White House by slipping his arms around his wife. He told the world 'We love each other'. Asked about their personal relationship in the wake of his affair with Mercy, Martin said, 'We are working hard. We love each other very much and we are working on it.' Many people anticipated the resignation of the President from office. He proved them wrong. He reacted positively to his circumstances.

The reality of winning life is demonstrated by your reaction to troubles. Read the biographies and autobiographies of successful people and you discover that each of these people have encountered opposition, discouragement, setbacks and personal misfortune. As you drive towards your destiny, you will hit potholes and take wrong turns. The only way to avoid them is never to leave your driveway. Troubles tend to come at an undetermined time. Its arrival cannot be pinpointed beforehand. It may be expected at anytime.

What are troubles?

Troubles are conditions of great distress, suffering, hardship or difficulty. There are different levels of human adversity and each level determines the urgency with which assistance must be sought and the manner in which you ought to proceed.

Professor Paul Welter has categorised adversities into five clearly defined areas.

1. PROBLEM: A question or issue which has a solution.

2. PREDICAMENT: A question or issue about which there is no essay or satisfactory solution.

3. CRISIS: A time of serious difficulty or danger. It is any event or series of events that threatens a person's well-being and interferes with his ability to cope with daily life. Such situations are often beyond his ability, sapping physical and emotional energy and leaving him disoriented. Crisis is a

very large predicament, usually short term, but requiring immediate and urgent action.

4. PANIC: A state of fear or apprehension in which a person becomes disoriented and irrational.

5. SHOCK: A dazed or numbed condition in which a person's mind may lapse for minutes or even hours.

According to Selwyn Hughes most of the issues we encounter in our daily lives are in the areas of problems and predicaments.

Causes of troubles

All troubles have an origin. This may be due to a simple or multiple factors. They may broadly be classified into three source groups.

1. Physical factor
2. Emotional factor
3. Spiritual factor

Everyone is subject to sickness, disease and infirmity. Some of these physical problems arise from inherited predisposition to certain sicknesses, others from injuries, accidents, climate, and lack of vitamins or environmental factors. These physical disharmonies greatly influence and bring misery to their victims.

We have psychological needs that can be narrowed down to three major groups.

1. The need to belong: assurance that we are desired, wanted and that in our absence we are missed.
2. The need for self-worth: we all need to feel a sense of personal worth and to feel valued, not so much for what we do, but for what we are.
3. The need to achieve: to be successful in at least one major aspect of life.

If these needs are not met then we probably develop a lifestyle which is overcome by constant fear or failure.

We were created to live in a relationship with God. Without that relationship there will always be some form of hunger, emptiness and a feeling that something is missing. Prince Charles of the United Kingdom spoke of his belief that, for all the advances of science, 'there remains deep in the soul, a persistent and unconscious anxiety that something is missing, some ingredient that makes life worth living.' Just as our physical and psychological needs cry out to be met, so do the needs of our spirit reach out to be fulfilled.

Symptoms of troubles

Dr D. J. Schwartz has listed nine symptoms of troubles.

1. A sense of bewilderment: 'I never felt this way before'
2. A sense of danger: 'I feel so scared something terrible is going to happen'
3. A sense of confusion: 'I can't think clearly – my mind doesn't seem to work'
4. A sense of impasse: 'I am stuck – nothing seems to help'
5. A sense of desperation: 'I have got to do something, but I don't know what'
6. A sense of apathy: ' Nothing can help me – what is the use of trying'
7. A sense of hopelessness: 'I can't cope by myself – please help me'
8. A sense of urgency: ' I need help now'
9. A sense of discomfort: ' I feel so miserable and unhappy'

It is acknowledged that a victim of adversity ponders on life's problems, worries about what will happen next and questions why it happened in the first place.

Lessons for life

No human life is without problems and I always do my best to view troubles as challenges and never lose hope, always learning a lesson from the creation story, which teaches us how the beginning of our universe was formless, empty and gloomy yet the spirit of God was hovering over the waters. (Genesis 1:1-2) Just as the spirit of God hovered on the formless and gloomy universe and also sent a heavenly visitor to accompany Shadrach, Meshach and Abednego during their time of great trial (Daniel 3:25), He is with me as I face new challenges or troubles in life.

Life is full of challenges. Without God it can be frightening. God promises us that He will never abandon us or fail to help us. (Joshua 1:5) By asking God to direct us we can conquer many of life's challenges. The man or woman who trusts in God and obeys His will is untouchable until God takes him or her. To trust God is to have immeasurable peace. God who delivered Shadrach, Meshach, Abednego, Daniel and many others will deliver you. Trust God in every situation. 'It is better to take refuge in the Lord than to trust in man.' (Psalm 118:8)

Problems are necessary evils

I always compare life to cars. Cars are equipped with an indicator stick or switch placed near the steering wheel directly in front of the driver; the indicators are a warning to other drivers that you are going to change direction. Hazard lights are flashing lights that warn other drivers that you or the car is in trouble, they indicate that something is wrong. Modern cars have an array of lights that indicate something is wrong with the car, low oil for instance or a flat battery. To ignore these warnings might ruin the car.

Drivers respond to all these various warning lights and do not become upset but automatically act on them. Our attention is not on the dashboard when we drive, particularly, although we may glance down at it from time to time to check the speedometer or petrol gauge. Our focus is through the windscreen, looking ahead at where we are going or where we want to go.

I have to be aware of the ups and downs in life – the troubles or problems – so that I can steer clear of them. Sometimes life's problems lead me to success if I am sensitive to them; sometimes, problems or troubles, like toothache, alert me that something is wrong, that I am in danger. Recognising the danger signals in life – the undesirable – I take immediate corrective action.

To forge towards the goal set before us there are some things that we need to learn on the way; some of which are lessons learnt during times of affliction. God allows things that are contrary to our desires to happen so that He can adjust us and improve our character so that we do not become weak in our faith, a spiritual wimp, not true to the Lord. Sufferings and afflictions cause us to grow more like Jesus. No one is exempt from crises in life, but He goes through the crisis with us.

The experienced teacher

One of my mentors is Nelson Mandela who rose to the highest position in South Africa after spending over 20 years in prison. He is recognised as one of the world's greatest leaders, having won the Nobel Peace Prize. Robben Island, where Nelson spent 18 of his 27 years in captivity, has been declared a World Heritage Site. Former inmate, Ahmed Kathrina, said: 'The message of Robben Island is a message of triumph, a message of victory, from prison to parliament to president.'

I have discovered from Mandela's life that 'everything that happens to us is our teacher. Everything that happens is either a blessing which is also a lesson or a lesson which is also a blessing. In life, it is not possible to order your life so perfectly as to avoid adversity. There will be times when we face problems. We don't always get what we want or desire straight away. In view of this, troubles cannot always be avoided and should not be feared; they should be embraced and overcome when they strike.

I have come to realise that trouble is an instructor not an obstacle; a teacher not a judge; an opportunity not a problem; a benefit and a blessing not a curse; a learning curve not an enemy. It will not kill me but will make me stronger. It matures and tests my commitment.

Every time something happens I ask myself: 'what can I learn from this? What benefit can I derive from this? What opportunities have been shown to me?' I do not question my ability, purpose in life or doubt my faith in God. I always resolve in advance that no matter the setback I will never give up.

To be successful you must have faith in God, believe in yourself and do what you must do when you should do it, and keep on doing it until you win. Nelson Mandela and many others overcame their own obstacles to write history.

Problems should not scare you

I have decided not to allow problems to scare me since I read Lennox Lewis' secret of success. He ended Britain's dismal sporting year on 15 November 1999 when he was crowned the country's first undisputed heavyweight champion of the century. He re-wrote 100 years of history by beating Evander Holyfield and put pride back into British sport after the nation's unsuccessful quest for world cups in football, rugby and cricket. A London newspaper made a notable remark, 'putting pride back into British sports: after ten years of effort Lennox Lewis is champion.' Lewis himself confirmed this by saying: 'It is a great feeling to be undisputed champion. It has been ten years of effort. I've been through trials and tribulations, different dramas and politics.'

Attaining destiny and living a fulfilled life takes boldness. It is a tenacity of life that does not swerve from a sense of direction even when confronting the greatest crisis of suffering. It is the state of not being intimidated by circumstances. It is an act of fearlessness and taking the bull by the horns.

In the face of the impossible challenges that lie before you, God is giving you the same instructions He gave Joshua, 'Be strong, sharp, determined and established.' (Joshua 1: 5-9) This is your standing obligation. Take hold of God's word and apply it to your own circumstances.

A twisted soul

There have been many trials in my life; many opportunities for bitterness to take root in me and grow. I have been betrayed and denied by friends but I always find it in my heart to forgive, so that disappointment may not grow to resentment; neither do I nurse grudges over past hurts. I know that, like a small root that grows into a great tree, bitterness when sprung up in my heart will overshadow my relationships. It defiles. (Hebrews 12:15) and brings with it jealousy, dissension and immorality. It will twist my soul and bring weariness to my life.

Think about this, 'It was a horrific act to witness when in 2008 a man drove his car straight at cheering spectators watching a parade in Holland – his target being the Dutch queen. Five died and 12 were injured. Why? The killer, allegedly, had just lost his job and was about to be evicted from his home.

Family, colleagues, friends and acquaintances at church and elsewhere may hurt you; the source of hurt may be in a trivial or a more sensitive issue. No matter the cause of the hurt, it is a well-known fact that the people most easily offended are those with low self-esteem; real 'digs' and 'cuts' often go by unnoticed by people with high self-esteem. 'A big strong man does not feel threatened by a small danger.' When feeling undeserving, doubtful of our own capabilities and holding a poor opinion of ourselves, we are prone to jealousy and hurt and become irritated at the drop of a hat.

We all need a certain amount of emotional toughness to protect us from hurt. Emotional strength comes from knowing who you are, your self–image and identity, and your security in God. You can cultivate a better and more adequate self-image so that every chance remark or innocent act will not threaten you. Trials and tribulations do not have to result in bitterness, they can make us better. An affliction can grow a character and can give us hope in the good God.

The power of past failures
John A. Schindler once said, 'Regardless of the omissions and commissions of the past, a person has to start in the present to acquire some maturity so that the future may be better

than the past.' Present and future successes depend on learning new habits and finding other ways of looking at old problems. There is no future in digging into the past.

I try not to have memories of past failures, unpleasant and painful experiences. I refuse to constantly 'dig them out'. It is good to remember our past mistakes or experiences to guide us in our future goals, for our errors, mistakes, failures and humiliations are necessary steps in the learning process, but they are a means to an end and not an end in themselves. If we consciously dwell upon our past failures, feel guilty about them, and keep on berating ourselves because of them, we make failure the ultimate goal in our memory.

Condemning and torturing ourselves over past failures destroys our chances of happiness in the present, we may then live in bitterness and resentment. The minute we change our minds and stop giving power to the past, the past with its mistakes loses power over us. F. Meyers was right when he said that many people carried around within themselves talents, abilities and powers which are locked in, unused, merely because of memories of past failures.

Acknowledging sincere regret for any wrong doing or hurt caused, by giving apologies, accepting the circumstances that seem stacked against us, with determination, wisdom and hope in God, we can rise up again.

Keep looking forward

The best way to drive a car is looking forward, fixing your attention on the road ahead and glancing up at the rear-view mirror. Using the rear-view mirror is essential if you want to change from one lane to another, turn off onto a side road or come to a stop. If our attention is always on the rear-view mirror and not on the road, an accident is guaranteed. In much the same way, we profit in life by looking forward rather than dwelling on what is behind us in the rear-view mirror; the negative things of the past.

There is always a reason to forget the past – calamities, people who have wronged us or deeply wounded us. We have all done things of which we are ashamed, and we live in the tension of what we have been and what we want to be. Because of our hope in God, we must let go of past guilt and look forward to what God will help us become. Realise that we are forgiven, and then move onto a life of faith and obedience – look forward to a fuller and more meaningful life. Think of growing in the knowledge of God by concentrating on your relationship with him. Look ahead to the joys and prosperity that are due to come. (Zechariah 7:1-13, 15) By all means look back on blessed memories from the past but meanwhile appreciate that the most blessed times are ahead – every day is a new life for a wise man.

Think about this, 'No man that puts his hand to the plough and looks back is fit for the service in the kingdom of God.' (Luke 9:62) Total dedication, not half-hearted commitment; focus, not picking and choosing or selectively following what suits, these are the keys to success. Accept the cross with the crown; count the cost and be willing to abandon everything else, even that which offers security. With our focus on God, we should allow nothing to distract us from living in a manner that is good and true.

Taking a proper attitude towards trouble

How can we come to terms with a story of a spurned boyfriend who shot at least three women dead and injured more than a dozen others at a packed fitness centre. The killer's girlfriend was said to be among the victims of the attack. The man then turned his gun on himself.

At times, we become aware that temptations and pressures, are slowly being carrying us away from good deeds. Difficulties and unfair circumstances are things we least expect to happen when they happen, arriving like strong winds that try to bring us to ruin, at such times we all need support and encouragement.

Face your problems because God is with you. A conflict that is suppressed and unresolved will manifest either as illness or as wrong patterns of behaviour. Assume personal responsibility and do not do stupid things. Remember, it is not so much what happens to us, but what we do with it that counts. Avoid self-pity and discipline your mind, for with the right mind set, every circumstance appears as an opportunity to add to experience and develop the character. Do not lose hope, for hope is what keeps you alive. Count it all as joy. (James 1:2) If you have deep-seated confidence that God knows what you are and what the result will be, adversities are viewed as sparing partners in the boxing ring of growth. Do not quit. Do not let the stinkers, those who want to suppress you or put you down, make you think of defeat. We need wisdom to see difficulties in their true light and to profit from them.

God is expert at bringing out the good in bad situations. The very same train of events set in motion by people for the worst possible motives can be used by God for our benefit. (Genesis 50:20) Fear nothing, for God is with us to help. (Isaiah 41:10) He will hold us by our right hand (Isaiah 41:13) and by walking in God's presence and trusting in His power we will avoid sinking into self-pity. Be assured that all the storms that threaten over our heads are beneath the feet of Jesus. (1 Corinthian 15:25-28)

Meeting challenges

Moreover, I have always believed that the best way to write history is to meet my challenges. You may already know the story of the great hymn writer, Haration G. Spafford. He was a successful businessman in Chicago in the 1800s. Spafford sold everything he had, to answer a calling to be a missionary in the Middle East. Staying behind to look after last minute business arrangements, he sent his family off in front of him. Their ship was wrecked en route and his children died but his wife survived. Despite this tragedy, his desire to be a missionary was not crushed and out of the tragedy he wrote the hymn 'When Peace Like a River Attendeth My Way', one of the greatest hymns of our time and a song of comfort and meaning to many.

The character of a person is measured by how they handle adversity. When you know God, tremendous suffering, great loss or dreadful disappointments are restored by Him. God can help a life recover and lift a person up to walk tall again.

Pat Mesiti has five steps to help you respond to and meet the challenges of life:

- Don't freak. Anger in times of trouble only blurs your vision. You cannot think well in a state of confusion and emotional instability.
- Define the problem. A problem defined is a problem half solved. Do this yourself or with the help of a wise and trusted person.
- Ask what caused the trouble. Unless you know what got you there, there

        is a chance you will end up there again.

- Develop a plan. Once you know your problem, develop a way to overcome it. Take action. Don't let things drift and don't just talk.

Problem solving

I've always believed that a good challenge presents new opportunity – opportunity to learn, to grow, to gain strength, or to reach a higher goal. There is a solution in every problem. Before possibility there shall be impossibility. It's not how we handle the good days that determines how well we do in life. It is how we handle the bad days. Almost everything we do involves problem-solving in one way or another. The way in which you solve problems may differentiate you, the winner, from them, the losers.

Stage1:
Identification:
Nature of problem
Define problem

↓

Stage 2:
Structuring
Observe, inspect
Fact find,
Develop clear picture

↓

Stage 3:
Looking for possible
Solutions:
Range of actions
No deep evaluation

↓

Stage 4:
Making a decision
Methodical analysis
Select solution

↓

Stage 5
Implementation
Carry out course of
action
Monitor
Seek feedback

↓

Stage 6
Monitoring/seeking
feedback
Review outcomes of
problem-solving

Problem-solving involves discovering a way out of some sort of difficulty. Helen Coult suggests a problem-solving plan, which is outlined here: first, define the problem; identify the underlying causes of the problem as well as the outward symptoms. Attempt to understand the problem as a whole – gathering all available facts about the situation – and ask yourself whether a similar problem has arisen before. If it has, past experiences might be able to help solve the problem. Develop a series of alternative solutions and do not accept the first one offered; evaluate all the alternatives. Ask whether they are compatible with your goals and abilities and select the best alternative solution. Problem-solving requires you to make decisions, so analyse the possible consequences of the decision and put in place a plan to cope with them. What are the potential obstacles? Who needs to be consulted? What is the timescale? Then implement your decision. Follow up and monitor the result of the decision, modifying it or taking remedial action if necessary. See the diagram above which illustrates the step–by-step approach to problem solving.

Trusting God with our lives means we consult him in every matter. Listen to Him; be willing to be corrected by His words; bring your decision to Him in prayer; use the Bible as your guide and follow His lead. He will straighten the path by guiding and protecting you. This does not mean there will not be problems, that we need not make decisions for ourselves or that we will not make mistakes.

The world is unfair. The world is finite and sin has twisted life, making it what God did not intend. He cares for us. (1 Peter 5:7) He hates wickedness and the suffering it causes. (Isaiah 55:8-9) He has a plan and will judge evil-doers in His time. Don't let the iniquities of life keep you from God. God is in the position to do you the most good. (Isaiah 40:28-29)

3

CYCLE OF DEFEAT

Justice's work has been sloppy and untidy of late. He misses deadlines. He sometimes comes in late and goes early. He seems to resent and takes perverse pleasure in thwarting his supervisor's intentions. Justice used to be hard working; in fact he was honorary treasurer of a local society which was full of praise for him. Eventually someone realised that he was worried about his marriage.

In our daily lives, we all face challenges, situations that can either make or break us. If we react improperly to the situation, it can rob us of the skills, control and ability that we ordinarily have to call upon. We then keep pondering on the problem and our inability. Finally, we get caught in a cycle of defeat.

The cycle of defeat is a recurring series of frustrated events in one's life. It is a state of uneasiness and adversity. One feels overcome, baffled or a loser in life. These events are challenges we either face directly or which affect our daily lives. Here is a summary of the cycle of defeat in its simplest form.

Table 1

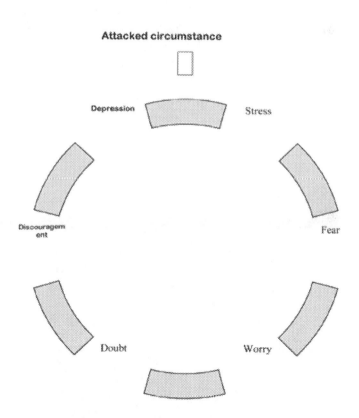

Attacked circumstance

Depression

Stress

Discouragement

Fear

Doubt

Worry

The battle begins with our daily circumstances – maybe in our most vulnerable areas – health, marriage, finances, employment, expectations, needs, relationships etc. Havoc is made of them if we lose control and appear to have no ability whatsoever. Losing control in our daily circumstances creates stresses that attack our entire body. It weakens our immune system and increases our susceptibility to almost every disease. Once we are defeated by stressful circumstances, our minds are bombarded with fear, worry and doubt. Our minds become filled with negative thoughts that enslave us.

Stress has become one of the great medical concerns in our present society. It has been linked to nervous breakdowns and heart attacks.

Symptoms of stress

- Change of personality or behaviour in an individual. This usually takes the form of a normally even-tempered person being irritable or aggressive
- Memory deterioration
- Stammering
- Emotional outburst
- May become obsessed with the trivial, want unattainable perfection or become very malicious or sarcastic
- Mental disorders including depression, anxiety, memory failure and phobias
- Accident proneness

- Often look and act stressed. Their fists are tightly clenched, their speech very tense and include none of the usual social phrases. They are always keeping their hands active.
- Exhibits the 'workaholic' symptoms of taking work home and putting in long hours
- Does not eat or sleep properly and may show obvious signs of weight loss and tiredness
- Drug abuse.

Physical conditions most commonly associated with stress are heart trouble, including heart attacks, angina pectoris and arrhythmia; circulatory illness including strokes, thrombosis and arteriosclerosis; skin disorders including lumbago and arthritis; back and joint trouble; breathing trouble, including asthma; sexual problems including impotence; increased susceptibility to colds and flu; migraines and cancers. In truth, stress related problems usually lead to mental and emotional deterioration, physical disability and pre-mature death.

Refuse to be discouraged in life and rejoice in its riches ...

Some people tend to perform better in adverse circumstances. The situation itself seems to empower them: gives them strength and ability that they do not ordinarily possess. As I have reflected on the issue of stress over the years. This truth stands out in my mind. None of the circumstances and troubles we face are responsible for creating stress. It is how we react to our circumstances and troubles that activate stress in our lives. If we are fearful, worried or doubtful that we shall come out of the adversity we are facing, we shall be overcome with stress. On the other hand, if we face these things knowing that we shall overcome the situation, our hearts and minds shall be filled with a peace that passes all understanding.

Are you caught up in stress? Then remember this: The first step to the successful treatment of stress is to break free from the cycle of defeat. The reality of a winning life is determined by a person's reaction when faced with problems. Many people are living in defeat because they have not recognised that they are using their own circumstances as weapons to defeat themselves. Regardless of your circumstances, stand firm, be strong, mighty and invincible. Always remember David. 'And David was greatly distressed because the men were talking of stoning him ... but he encouraged himself in the Lord his God.' (1 Samuel 30:6)

Live for today because tomorrow will definitely take care of himself

Marcus was a successful businessman. He hanged himself in despair in the wake of the Credit Crunch. He saw his business collapse and his property about to be repossessed. He could not see it getting better. He couldn't see any way of making it work. He believed no one cared about him.

The Bible forewarns us not to fret or suffer anxiety about anything, yet we reject such precious counsel. No doubt, as Dale Carnegie comments, one of the most appalling indictments of our present way of life is that at one time half of all the beds in our hospitals were reserved for patients with nervous and mental troubles, patients who had collapsed under the crushing burden of accumulated yesterdays and fearful tomorrows. Yet the vast majority of those people could have avoided hospital, could have led happy, useful lives, if they had only heeded the words of Jesus: 'Have no anxiety about tomorrow.'

Three reasons to not worry

- Worry cannot change the body;
- God's providence is over all creation, not only birds and plants that never buy, sell, manufacture or labour;
- Worry is useless and sinful and must not be tolerated.

A British millionaire shot dead his wife in their Spanish home before turning the gun on himself. David killed wife Heather, aged in her mid -50s, as she slept. The 70 year old put out water and food for their pet dog and cat, left his identification on a table and the front door open before committing suicide. 'He appears to have planned the crime meticulously', a police spokesman said.

Worry is sinful and produces fear; it is a disease that causes other ills. Borrowing troubles that cannot be paid off; brooding over what may not happen create trouble, misery and death. Worry is a burden borrowed from tomorrow which others should be carrying; a weight that kills prematurely. Worry is both mental and physical suicide; a grave-digger without sympathy. Worry is needless and time wasting. The effort of worrying could be spent on worthwhile activities. Worry robs the heavenly Father of our never-failing faith, peace and trust. Worry is a stumbling block, a disgrace to God, and Christians should not indulge in it. Anxiety over what is nothing today and less tomorrow anticipates troubles which seldom come to those who trust God. Worry is tormenting oneself over something that will likely be a blessing if it arises. Worry means you live like an orphan without a heavenly Father. It is a crime against God, man, nature and better judgment. Worry is a mental cruelty and causes others pain; it is foolishness to worry about what is going to happen when it cannot be stopped by worry. The worst does not happen; there is nothing to worry about; should adversity come, one may still be victorious by trusting God.

Live for today by faith

If you are insecure, angry and self-conscious you will appear uncomfortable in your own skin. Mental and physical self-consciousness can be overcome by staying focused. We are all complex, but some people mask and manage their insecurities and anxieties better than others. Stop worrying and live by faith:

- Remember and trust God's promises (Exodus 14:13)
- Place your cares in the hands of Jesus (Philippians 4:6)
- Find relief from fear in the promise of salvation (Psalm 62:6)
- Focus on Kingdom priorities (Matthew 6:27)

Focus on a great goal and stop being worried about how you look, what others will think of you or whether you are going to fail. Look for the opportunity to grow, not the problem. Think in terms of improvement.

Our heavenly Father will not disappoint us. He will not give us anything that is bad. He will give 'good things' to those who ask Him. He knows our needs and He knows how to meet those needs with His wisdom and compassion. God would not forget nor forsake us. We can be certain that the one who gave us spiritual birth will never abandon or fail us. He is an eager provider and protector of His children. He will carry us all the way to our destination. 'He who did not spare His own Son but gave

Him up for us all, how will He not also with Him graciously give us all things?' (Romans 8:32) 'Set your mind on things above, not on earthly things.' (Colossians 3:2) Jesus is our hope in times of personal calamities and storms. He is the source of hope in times of crisis. In the hour of crisis, there is just no alternative to Jesus, although supplements such as the music, literature, art, nature and relationships can help. Time heals but not as wonderfully as Jesus. Remember always that 'the extent to which you allow worry access into your mind and control of your thoughts is the degree to which it destroys you'.

Fear not, for you were born with the spirit to succeed Marcus, a new striker, has joined the Unity Football club. He was welcomed with cries of 'Here he comes, the striker-in-waiting'. The assistant coach and some of the fans warned Jimmy, the old striker, however, that Marcus' arrival could 'spark a striker-coup' and that then he would be replaced. He was warned to watch his back. While I am not holding a brief for Jimmy, my concern is that if Jimmy fills his mind with this 'striker-coup ideology' fear will engulf him. And his point of fear will be his point of failure in football. For wherever fear begins, faith and victory end.

There are six basic fears that confront us. We may suffer from one or a combination of them at one time or another, writes Napoleon Hill.
- The fear of poverty

- The fear of criticism
- The fear of ill-health
- The fear of loss of love of someone
- The fear of old age
- The fear of death

More than any other single lesson, my experiences have conspired to teach me the value of boldness and not to give way to fear. I have come to realise that fear is the number one enemy of success. It stops people from capitalising on opportunities. It wears down physical utility and prevents people from getting what they want from life. It steals people's faith and confidence from their hearts. It is the springboard for the worry and negative thoughts that enslave us. As fear grips our mind, we begin to worry about our circumstances. Night and day our minds are in a constant state of turmoil. A story is told of Martyn, a successful farmer in Britain, who hanged himself in despair at the crisis of Britain's crippled agricultural industry in 1999. Martyn saw his annual net income halved to £5,000 in just one year. He could not see it getting any better. He could not see any way of making it work. He believed no one cared about farmers.

Fear of all kinds has magnifying eyes, a quick ear and wings. It is both bondage and a prison of the heart. It is always better to pass a danger zone once than be always in fear, for it is said 'better a fearful end than fear without end'. We must always isolate our fear by determining exactly what we are afraid of. Ask yourself: 'What is the worst that could possibly happen?' Prepare to accept it if you have to. Then calmly proceed to improve on the worst. . In truth, there is no remedy for fear but to cut off the head. The weapon to cut through the head is faith in God. God has promised to defend us and to be our great reward. (Genesis 15:1) When we fear what lies ahead, we must always remember that God will stay with us through difficult times and that He has promised us great reward. This one thing I always do. I put thoughts about my own weaknesses behind me and focus instead on the strengths of God. I am what God says I am. I can do what God says I can do and I have what God says I have. My faith in God is the light in the tunnel which pushes fear out. 'I have no fear of sudden disaster ... that overtakes the wicked.' (Proverbs 3:25) 'No weapon forged against me will prevail ...'. (Isaiah 54:17)

Inner doubts turn molehills into mountains, but faith moves them

When the going becomes tough I always ponder the cause of the Israelites' long wandering on the wilderness. God specifically promised Israel, through Moses, that He would drive out all their enemies and give them the land of Canaan as inheritance. Yet, when they come to Kadesh-Barnea and saw the giants in the land, they were afraid. Instead of listening to God's voice, they listened to the voices of the spies who said the people were 'giants' and were more powerful than them. Their minds were filled with doubt. It was the cause of their hardened hearts which ultimately brought their destruction.

A mind filled with doubt conveys the image of a divided mind torn in two directions. This individual is divided between the desire to say 'Yes, I can do it' and the desire to say, 'No, I can't do it'; the overbearing inclination is to say 'no' as is an inner unwillingness to stick with a vision. He who doubts does not offer a steady hand or heart to receive inspiration and is deficient in his ability to attain any fixed goals. The doubter lacks a firm inner will of his own and is totally 'untrustworthy' in terms of getting the job done as he lacks the determined perseverance to stay on a certain course. Power does not dwell in a personality so unstable and unable to carry out a determined course of action. (James 1: 6-7)

We will prosper if we learn to develop a whole-hearted attitude of a full and unquestioning committal to God who gives us the strength to do whatsoever we want to do. "Have faith in God' Jesus answered.' (Mark 11:22)

Refuse to be discouraged in life

Very often in my life, the odds of surviving are stacked against me. But I have this philosophy, 'If you have that frame of a dream down inside you somewhere, thank God for it, and do something about it. And do not let anyone else blow it out.' (Rich Devos) For this reason, I am always determined to call the shots for the challenges in my life. I refuse to be discouraged in life. Think about this, 'The Starr report accused President Clinton of 11 crimes for which he was to be impeached, including perjury, obstructing justice, and witness-tampering and abuse of power. He stood trial. Media coverage led viewers to expect 'angry' and 'evasive' answers to the video camera. In fact he was composed and eloquent in his answers. Many people anticipated his resignation, a word that is not in his vocabulary. He declared that he would remain in office until the end of his term. He was acquitted of perjury and obstruction of justice. He was still in business.

What stops you from fulfilling your vision? Discouragement is a real handicap whose symptoms include loss of hope, zeal, enthusiasm and confidence in life. A fear to continue, take risks or perform a task may set in. It associates itself with apathy and a lack of belief. Discouraged people complain, murmur, moan and blame others for their circumstances. They spread words of discouragement. With this bad attitude, they dispirit others by sowing seeds of fear, worry and discouragement.

Life expands in proportion to courage. It discouragement buries principle. In a state of discouragement, one doesn't have the ability to see or the conviction to pursue a course of action. Discouraged people may think often of death, suicide or resignation. They feel worthless. The lack of courage among us today explains the number of failures in our lives. Regardless of our circumstances, we must stand firm, be strong, mighty and invincible. We can make the decision to not be discouraged in life and remember that 'If God is for us, who can be against us?' and 'We can do all things through Christ that strengthens us.' (Philippians 4:13)

If successful do not crow; if defeated do not croak

There is also this major roadblock ahead of us all. We can pretend it isn't out there, that in some miraculous way, we'll turn off onto this side of the road. It waits for us all. Think about the story of James. 'Every day of my life', says 30 year old James, 'I have fought this emotional and mental illness. I felt so worthless when I was young that I tore up my childhood photographs. I didn't even think I was worth remembering.'

Depression is a state of sadness where life is suddenly darkened by a cloud of regret for no apparent reason. Depression alters emotions and moods, so those suffering depression often become withdrawn and unhappy, and often smoke and drink too much alcohol too. Many depressed people become addicted to drugs and some have eating problems, and often lack motivation and energy. Depression makes people lose interest in normal daily activities, including sex, and isolates them from their family. They feel worthless and then guilty, lose confidence, and often have difficulty concentrating. They may think often about death or suicide.

The cycle of life has mixed blessings. There are days of frustration and days of joy; we are all in peril of becoming depressed by one and elated by another. Some measure of depression is very normal, whether it is in anticipation of a great achievement, regret that our ideals and goals are not realised, or because people we trust have disappointed us.

We often wish we could escape our troubles, the cycle of grief, loss, sorrow, and failure that many endure; even small daily frustrations wear us down. God promises to be close to those that are broken at heart; (Isaiah 57:15; Psalm 34:18) to be our source of power, courage and wisdom, helping us through our problems. At any time of the day we can approach God to hear our prayer for He can help us cope with distressing feelings and circumstances. (Psalm 65:2) 'We must pour out our hearts to him.' (Philippians 4:6-7)

Are you caught in a cycle of defeat? Remember these:

'Though the fig tree does not bud and there are no grapes on the vines, though the olive crop fails and the fields produce no food, though there are no sheep in the pen and no cattle in the stalls, yet I will rejoice in life. I shall never be shaken. I refuse to be discouraged in life. I shall never allow myself to be discouraged'.

The first step to a successful life is to break the yoke of the cycle of defeat. Cultivate the habit of conquering the negative forces of worry, anxiety, fear, doubt, discouragement, depression and stress.

The power of choice

Think about this, as early as childhood we come to terms with the basic problem of economics. We cannot have all the things we want. Economists describe this basic problem as people's wants being unlimited while the means they have of satisfying their wants are limited. Since we cannot satisfy all our wants, we have to choose between them. Everyone, rich or poor, has to make choices. God allowed the first man, Adam, responsibility for the garden and told him not to eat from the tree of the knowledge of good and evil. Rather than physically preventing him from eating from it, God gave him the freedom to choose. Without choice, Adam would have been like a prisoner and his obedience would have been hollow.

God still gives us choice. Choice is humankind's ultimate freedom and greatest power. It is our birthright, the power to think whatever we choose to allow into our head. Using the power of choice to make decisions, we determine our future. We cannot eat our cake and have it. We cannot enjoy both the privilege of choice and the choice of consequences at the same time. As Colin Turner tells us, the consequences of our actions are always predetermined by the principle of cause and effect. Frustration comes about through wanting both the pleasures and prestige of one choice and the consequences of another. It means we should not blame circumstances for any situation we find ourselves in. We are the sum total of our choices made to date. The two trees at Eden provided an exercise in choice for Adam and Eve, with rewards for choosing to obey and sad consequences for choosing to disobey.

When we make choices we obviously risk losing but we also stand to win. It is better to attempt great things even if we fail sometimes than to stand on the sidelines of life. The power of choice is unique to us and a privilege. We alone can open or shut the door to our own future. Making the right choices is a key to a successful life. While wrong choices may cause us pain they nevertheless help us to learn and grow and make better choices in the future. Living with the consequences of our choices teaches us to think and choose more carefully.

The choice is yours
A time comes when we have to choose who or what will control our destiny. 'We cannot have it both ways' 'you cannot sell the cow and sup the milk'. The essence of life is in decision

making, the process of choosing one course among various courses of action in order to achieve a goal. Our choices are very important because the right choices put us on the road to victory. Bob Gass counsels that 50 per cent of success is in knowing what you have to give up in order for your goal to be reached. Apparently, successful people pay the price that mediocre people are not willing to pay. The value of our dreams is determined by what we are willing to give up, otherwise it is only talk.

We may be caught in a cycle of defeat irrespective of who we are, but we nevertheless always have a choice. We may choose to focus or refuse to focus on the circumstances. We may choose to look at the size of the impossible circumstances and dwell on discouraging moments, or look at the ability of God and concentrate on His solution to the problem. We have a choice to take counsel of our fears and underestimate God and our abilities, or focus on God and underestimate the nature of the difficulty.

Regardless of what others decided, Joshua made a commitment to God and he was willing to set the example of living by that decision. The way we live shows others the strength of our commitment. Will your focus be on God or on your limited personality or circumstances in life? The choice is yours.

Count your blessings

For me, whatever the wind blows my way, I am determined to count my blessings. I think of all that I have to be grateful to God for and have cultivated the habit of looking on the best side of life. Progress is always fuelled by positive, optimistic thinking. We must turn to God. We must never ever forget anything he has done for us. (Psalm 103:1-6) To help not forget God, we must review, continue reading and remain listening to God's Word. Keep on glorifying God by being His witness, get acquainted with what He wants done and then do it. We must always remember that gratitude is the least of virtues, but ingratitude is the worst of vices. King David never ever forgot anything God had done for him. Listen to him, 'Bless God, O my soul, and do not forget all His doings.' (Psalm 103:2) Appreciation is the key that opens up many avenues for expressing our thanks to God. We must not forget little kindnesses and fail to remember small faults.

Resist the failure syndrome

There are heights we can reach if we can only whip our past failures and press forward to focus on the goal we have set before us. There is victory in every circumstance we face, but it is not automatic.

I believe in patience and endurance. At times waiting a little longer shall make a difference in our lives. We are defeated when we become weary and 'faint' in our minds. Regardless of how long I have to wait for a breakthrough in my circumstances ... regardless of the pain and heartache I feel ... perseverance has been my major essential weapon.

Contentment

I am content in whatever circumstance I am in. I know this very well; 'My attitude creates the environment' Mr Loser is always waiting for others to do something instead of realising he is responsible for his own life.

My key to life is simple. 'I am content with every situation'. I know what it is to be in need and what it is to have in abundance. I have learnt the secret of being content in any and every situation, whether well fed or hungry. And I know that 'contentment is a rare bird, as Martin Luther once said, 'but sings sweetly in the breast'. Content makes poor men rich. Discontent makes rich people poor'

Contentment is not just having everything you want – a better house, more money, looking beautiful or human relationships. These things do not bring contentment, only a desire for more. This does not imply that there is something wrong with having food or possessions.

4

THE TRAPS OF LIFE

'Multi live catch repeating mouse trap: simple to use, easy to clean, strong and safe for children, pets and for the captured mice, No Poison, No Kill, Humane Live Catch', a company puts up an advert. Here's how the multi live catch repeating mouse trap works, two side entrance openings conceal an inclined slope that the mice are enticed into by their own curiosity, other captured mice or some form of bait or attractant. As the mouse walks up the incline the weight of the mouse tips it into the trap at the same instance closing the door and resetting the trap for the next mouse to enter. Place the multi live catch repeating mouse trap flat on the floor against the wall or skirting with the openings adjacent to the wall. Mice run from one safety point to another, they'll run along the wall and into the opening in the trap and be enticed into the trap and safely caught. Trapped mice attract other mice; soon you may catch the whole family, up to thirty mice, with out resetting the trap, safely without harming the mice. Bait with a quarter inch slice of Snicker bar placed in the centre of the trap, in hot dry weather a jam jar lid filled with water works as excellent bait. Close the lid and place a small book over the transparent cover to exclude the light. If the mice won't go in, try leaving the lid open until the mice start eating the bait, then re-bait and close the lid.

Failure, like 'multi live catch trap' captures its victims through entrance openings concealed that entice us into by our own curiosity, while some are captured in some form of bait or attractant. Life's common traps are:

- Offence
- Hopelessness
- Resentment
- Problems
- Bitterness
- Pride
- Over-confidence
- Superstition
- Curse
- Oppression

Offence

The citizens of Nazareth, the home town of Jesus became offended because of familiarity. They refused to believe that someone they had known from childhood could be anointed by God to do miracles. Jesus could not do any mighty miracles among them except to place his hands on a few sick people and heal them. (Mark 6:1-6) It's obvious that offence has been a bait that traps and imprisons us.

Offence can be anything that arouses prejudice or becomes a hindrance to others, or causes them to fall by the way. It's a trap, bait, snare that entices us to sin. Offences and hurts are not intentional.

Offence makes us focus on ourselves and distracts us from the promises of God. When our focus is diverted from the word of God, we are left to solve our problems with our limited understanding and natural reasoning. Offence hinders the power of God to both remove and destroy the burdens with which the enemy tries to overload us. Offences develop anger, resentment, bitterness and hatred.

No matter what is done against me or what wrong choice other people make, I never allow anything to hurt or offend me. I avoid offence in my life by guarding my heart. (Proverbs 4:23) When our hearts are left unguarded – open to every assault that comes our way – we are certain to be a vulnerable target for the enemy.

It's our responsibility to guard our heart from those who would wound it by keeping God's word before our eyes and in our hearts. It should penetrate deep within our heart. (Proverbs 4:21; Psalm 119:165) We must choose to keep our eyes fixed on the promise of God, regardless of what is going on around us.

Hopelessness

A city banker threw himself to his death in front of a rush hour train hours before a dinner date with his wife. Jonas had apparently been coping well with the pressures of his job, and his death was described as a 'mystery'. When he leapt into the path of the train, despite not being known as a heavy drinker, was nearly five times over the 'legal driving limit'.

In one way or another, at any given time, most of us face some frustration, hopelessness and anger. We may not measure up to our goals. We become lose hope because of these disappointments – a state of life in which whenever success seems within out grasp, something happens to defeat us. We thereby conceive ourselves to be unworthy, incompetent, inferior, having no right to succeed or to enjoy better things.

No matter how hopeless life may seem to be, feeling discontented is never the answer. Life would never have pity on you and meet you half way. It would rather become fertile soil for defeated life. If you are going through a period of hopelessness remember always that every human being at a point in this life suffers some form of frustration. All our decisions cannot be satisfied immediately. We must learn to accept the fact that perfection in deeds and image is not necessary or required and that approximations are good enough for all practical purposes. We are not perfect. We must learn to tolerate a certain amount of frustration. As goals are achieved when they are realistic and measurable, we must set goals that are specific.

At times of hopelessness we all need support and encouragement. God could restore our hope. He wants to give us a future and a hop.e (Jeremiah 29:11) If we hope in God, we will not be disappointed. If our hope is contained and centred on the promises of God, we are not going to be ashamed. He has called us to hope. It's a glorious inheritance. (Ephesians 1:18)

Resentment

Nick resigned as a general manager of Kings Cross Textile Ltd. He felt the chief executive was ungrateful. He moaned that management did nothing to keep him in the company. Nick was very resentful because he believed the company should be dedicated to make him happy.The world is full of people, like Nick, who want to pass the buck. They are looking everywhere to justify their failure and thereby run away from responsibility. They try to 'prove' their case before the court of life, writes Maxwell Maltz.

We are in such crises due to our own emotional response to issues. It's not caused by other persons, events or circumstances. In life, no one owes anyone anything. Each and every one should be an actor rather than a passive recipient of life. We must go after our own goals. We are responsible for our own success and happiness. We cannot justify our own failure by explaining it in terms of unfair treatment and injustice or re-fighting events in the past.

Resentment is a deadly poison to the spirit and our energy. It makes us picture ourselves as victims of life. It goes with inferior self-image. It positions us in sad circumstance. It makes us prostrate in darkness on the ground. Hard pressed, perplexed, persecuted, and struck down. Nevertheless a light is piercing the gloom. 'Arise and shed forth light, for your light has come'. Surely we should get to our feet and reflect God's glory?

Bitterness

A young man stabbed an elderly man to death. It was a brutal killing. The police were puzzled. What was the motive? They asked the boy. 'Did you know him?' 'No'. 'Did he talk to you?' 'No'. 'Have you ever met him before?' 'No'. 'Did he hurt you?' 'No'. 'Did he hurt your parents?' 'No'.

Hours later the 16 year old broke down and cried and began to tell all. His father declared him 'good-for-nothing' while bragging about his other brother.

Bitterness against someone who has wronged us is 'an evil cancer' within us and will eventually destroy us. Like a small root that grows into a great tree, bitterness springs up in our hearts and overshadows virtues. It comes when we allow disappointment to grow into resentment, or when we nurse grudges over past hurts.

Bitterness brings with it jealousy, dissension, and immorality. Think about this, 'Cain killed his brother, Abel, when God accepted Abel's offering and not his. (Genesis 4: 1-4) Cain's jealous anger drove him to murder.

People who are morally upright expose and shame those who aren't. Don't let a 'bitter root' grow in you. Make a list of the people who have wronged or hurt you. Write down what you have done to hurt others. Throw the list in the bin or burn it. Forgive the offenders. Think about God's love for you and do the same to your brother. 'While we were still sinners Christ died for us'. (Romans 5:8) If God loved you when you were a rebel, he can surely strengthen you, now that you love him, to love anyone who hurt you.

Pride

Glad to be a good girl. Leona Lewis has hit back at critics who mock her squeaky clean image, 'I've been brought up properly by my parents and I'm respectful. Is it bad to be a good person? I don't think so', the 24-year-old singer said. It is tempting to exalt ourselves by speaking well of ourselves, taking ourselves too seriously and think too highly of ourselves. This is pride. It frequently goes with educational advantages, achievement, fame, power, wealth, race, religion and nationality.

Pride sees only the shortcomings in others but is blind to its own weaknesses and shortcomings. It is not only fully conscious of its own good points but imagines it has many that it does not possess. It is disruptive and spurs rivalry and competition instead of harmony and cooperation. It causes us to refuse to admit a wrong and to refuse to forgive and forget. It has caused many divorces and deliquencies because it blinds patience, understanding and fans exasperation and rebellion. In the spiritual sphere, it makes submission to authority irksome and makes an opponent of God. It blinds our understanding to the scripture and causes us to oppose the divine will of God.

In truth, pride is before a crash and a haughty spirit before stumbling. (Proverbs 16:18) Pride goes before, and shame follows after. It is a flower that grows in the Devil's garden and when joined with many virtues, chokes them all.

Evaluating ourselves by the worldly standards of success in achievement can cause us to think much about our worth in the eyes of others and thus mess our true value in God's eyes. Our true identity is in Christ. In him we are valuable and capable of worthy service. God opposes the proud but gives grace to the humble. (1 Peter 5:5) Wisdom also hates pride and self-exaltation. (Psalm 8:13) Let not the rich man brag about himself because of his riches, counsels the Holy Scriptures.

Over-confidence

Victor Hugo writes of the over-confidence that Napoleon displayed before the battle of Waterloo. He even sent a dispatch to Paris to chronicle that the battle was gained when victory was not truly within his grasp. His defeat at Waterloo had been partially attributed to his overconfidence. He did not show his usual care and thoroughness in his orders, nor his usual broad judgment in execution. Today 'Waterloo' has become proverbial for 'a decisive or disastrous defeat or reversal'.

The future is unknown and uncertain. There are many things, such as weather and health, over which we might not be able to exercise control. At all times and in all our ways we need to take notice of God. (James 4:15; Proverbs 3:6)

Over-confidence may cause us to act with poor judgment. 'This is easy'. How often do we utter such words when we are faced with a new task, job or assignment. There is always the temptation of thinking that we know so much better what should be done than those who have had much experience at it.

We must be on guard against over-confidence. Wisdom is with the modest ones. When pride comes, then comes disgrace. (Proverbs 11:2) Pride increases our enemies, but puts our friends to flight. Pride, joined with many virtues, chokes them all. It's a sworn enemy to content. Over-confidence causes us to fail to prepare properly – in marriages, jobs, tasks etc – consequently the number of emotional immaturities, divorces, accidents, glittering generalities, inaccuracies and failures, writes a tabloid. Over-confidence is always ill-advised. Caution and modesty and looking to God for help are the course of wisdom

Curse
Daniel and Sam are very good friends. They have the same background, ability, and purpose in life. While Sam is overshadowed by failure and frustration, Daniel walks in the light of success and fulfilment. Derek Prince concluded the story by saying that there are forces at work in their lives defining their destiny. This divine impediment or enablement to failure or success is called curse and blessing.

A curse is like a long, evil arm stretched out from the past. It rests upon people with dark oppressive forces that inhibit the full expression of their personality. It has a tripping effect on its victims. Such people live in a chronic state of uncertainty and stumbling. They become shattered when they are within reach of attaining some long-sought goal. In truth there seems to be no natural or logical reason to explain why success eludes them.

Derek Prince has compiled a list of seven problems indicating that a curse is at work especially when several of the problems are present or when any one of them tend to recur repeatedly. Mental or emotional breakdown; repeated or chronic sicknesses especially if hereditary; barrenness and a tendency to miscarry or related female problems; breakdown of marriage and family alienation; continuing financial insufficiency; being 'accident-prone' and a history of suicides and unnatural or untimely deaths.

God has set before us a choice between blessings and curses. (Deuteronomy 11:26; Deuteronomy 30:19; John 3:16) To live for ourselves is to travel on a dead end road, but to choose God's way is to receive blessings.

Superstition
There is luck in odd numbers. 'The third is a charm. All things thrive at thrice, lucky at life, unlucky in love. When a picture leaves

the wall, someone then receives a call'. In our contemporary world, people are preoccupied with star signs, palm reading, the zodiac and the like. Many people buy a newspaper just to ascertain their future from star signs. 'I am Scorpio, Aquarius and the like' is increasingly becoming very popular even among believers. Beliefs that forces other than God have powers over our lives are superstitions or astrology.

Superstition should be eradicated from our lives. When it rules over our lives, it makes us refuse to alter daily routines or forces us to avoid people with certain characteristics, for example certain names and dates of birth. People in the grip of superstition often suffer from distorted outlooks, they lose the ability to connect with other people and thereby lose awaited opportunity. It also distracts them from focussing on God's supreme power, which makes it idolatrous.

As Christians, we cannot take superstition seriously. We have to forget these signs and trust in God. God is not prepared for the humiliation of having himself compared with someone else. He wants to feel unique, distinguished and special. He must be accorded primacy.

Oppression
To be oppressed means to be under subjection by a force stronger than you are. It is being tortured by certain forces that are beyond your control. It is a state of captivity in which

you rely on your enemy for survival, writes Dr Daniel Olukoya.

It takes different forms: physical, mental, spiritual, marital, financial, career, dream, verbal, emotional, withcraft, inherited, forced, conscious and unconscious. You may experience one or a combination of the folowing: You may realise that something is not right in your body but cannot pin point it. No joy in your marriage or relationship. Every night is another battle ground of war with forces that are stronger than you are. Your tongue is a snare. Most of the time you feel sad or downcast for no obvious reason. Ancestral or generational disability or sickness.

Oppression is a demon assigned by the Devil to trap and cage you, writes Dr Daniel Olukoya. It is the foundation for difficulties, frustrations, hardships and unbearable sufferings. It makes a wise man mad and a gift that destroys the heart. (Ecclesiastes 7:7) It is a tool of the Devil who comes to kill, condemn and steal. (John 10:10) It makes havoc out of your circumstances. It can remove your alertness and make you lose your focus. An oppressed person may doubt God.

In truth, as Christians, oppression is meant to be far from us. (Psalm 42:9; Isaiah 54:14) God has plans and purpose for our lives. God's plan for us is always for good. Unknown plans can be frightening, but when the plans belong to

God, we can rest assured that we can expect something marvelous. He cares about what we do and the details of our lives.

Our heavenly father's loving purpose for us include

- He is always willing to answer prayer (Isaiah 65:24; Matthew 7:1)
- He longs for us to be His children (Jeremiah 3:19)
- He delights to show mercy (Micah 7:18)
- He purposes that we may have life and have it to the full (John 10:10)
- He wants to set us free from fear (John 14:1; Psalm 118:5-9)
- He desires to give us an eternal home (John 14:2-3)
- He wants all mankind to be saved (1 Timothy 2:3-4)
- He wants to take care of our needs (1 Peter 5:7)

God cares. We can be certain that the one who gave us spiritual birth will never abandon us or fail us. Before we call he will answer, while we are still speaking he will hear'. (Isaiah 65:24)

5

ACHILLES' HEEL

Achilles was one of the bravest Greek warriors in the Trojan War. He was invincible except for his heel, and that was where Paris, son of Priam, the king of Troy, shot an arrow to kill him. Flesh is frail. We all have a weak spot, 'our Achilles' heel', which makes us vulnerable and fatal especially if we are caught unawares. Man is not an angel. We have the defects of our qualities. We are born in sin, and our sinful and imperfect nature can easily overpower our resolve to do good.

We all have evil desires

A pregnant woman stabbed to death in a random attack was one of the greatest people anyone could hope to meet, one of her friends said. Seven months pregnant, Claire died after she was stabbed on the back by a stranger as she walked to work. Her unborn daughter, whom she had already named Abigail also died later.

All evil deeds are blamed on the Devil or Satan, a word meaning 'to set one against another'. Christians believe that the Devil is against God and tries to tempt people away from God. Nevertheless, the evil deeds that are prevalent in society are not all the direct works of the Devil. The Devil 'operates' on our evil desires.

Our evil desires can be grouped into four: Works of the sexual realm; Works in the Spiritual realm; Works of the Social realm and Works in the realm of self-indulgence.

Works of the sexual realm are immorality, impunity and sensuality. Immorality is fornication and adultery. Impunity thinks about immorality all the time. Sensuality is sexual irresponsibility. We become blatantly open with immorality. It is immorality that parades itself without shame, hanging depravity out for the whole world to see. Works in the Spiritual realm are idolatry and sorcery. It is worshipping anything other than the true God. We worship possessions, positions, status symbols and even sex. Sorcery denotes the use of drugs in worship. Works of the social realm are works of the flesh that strike at unity – enmities, hatred, hostility towards one another, strife – outbursts of anger, disputes and selfish ambition, dissensions, jealousy and envy. Social sins bring division to a point that people have to choose between two parties. Jealousy and envy resents what others possess and wants to take what belongs to others. Works in the realm of self-indulgence are drunkenness and carousing

The 'spirit' of the last days (2 Timothy 3:1-3) also lures us into sin. With our spiritual priorities slipping by slacking off in Bible study, prayer and congregational fellowship, loss of sense of urgency in our spiritual warfare, easily irritated when others do or say something not to our liking, difficult to get along with others, standards brought down along with the world, reluctance to pursue spiritual goals, finding counsel hard to accept and feel that others are always picking on us, we are developing a low hedge which Satan and his horde of demons can easily leap over.

In the Christian life, we battle against powerful evil forces of fallen angels headed by Satan, who is a vicious fighter. (1 Peter 5:8) These forces are not 'flesh and blood'. They are not mere fantasies but real. They have become our enemies since we believed in Jesus Christ and they are trying every device to turn us away from Christ back to sin. They are very cunning in their schemes.

Think about this, 'even though the spiritual armour of God is of the finest quality and a source of security for us, we must not take things for granted because the supposedly invincible Achilles was defeated. He had a weak spot'. Where the hedge is lowest, men may soonest go over. The thread breaks where it is weakest. Lions attack sick, young or staggering animals. They choose victims who are alone or not alert. So if you think you are standing firm be careful that you don't fall. (1 Corinthians 10:12)

No Christian can have the fullness of the Spirit of God if he does not deal with the flesh. We must strive to crucify the flesh. (Galatians 5:24) The good news is that our old nature was crucified with Jesus on the cross. (Romans 6:6) Now it is necessary for us to appropriate this by faith.

The battlefield

Today people still say 'he has met his Waterloo' when someone who has been successful for a time is at last defeated. Waterloo was the final defeat of the French emperor Napoleon 1, who had returned from his exile on the island of Elba and marched with an army across France, determined once again to make himself the master of Europe. The battle that prevented him from accomplishing this was fought on 18 June 1815, and was centered on the village of Mont St. Jean in Belgium. Waterloo was another village to the north of the battlefield. Satan is at war with humanity and the main battlefield is our senses, especially our mind, eyes and mouth. He traps us through what we watch, say and hear.

The mind

The mind is recognised as the place where the emotions, desires, perceptions, thoughts, understanding, reasoning powers, conscience, intentions, the will and imaginations reside. It stands for man's entire mental and moral activity ... the inner man. All the strategies Satan has developed and is using against us today are directed toward our minds. Our minds are his major point of attack and it is there... in our minds... the battle must be fought and won, writes Morris Cerrulo.

He corrupts our mind so that he will be able to gain control of our wills. As a 'prince of this world' he has the ability to 'blind' the minds of people from seeing the truth of the gospel of Christ. Once he has blinded our minds, he is able to take us captive to do his will.

We must programme our minds with thoughts that are true, noble, right, pure, lovely, ad-mirable, excellent, and praiseworthy. (Philip-pians 4:8) We must examine what we put into our minds through television, books, conver-sations, films and magazines; replace harm-ful input with wholesale material and always remember that the extent to which we allow Satan to have access into our minds and to control our thoughts is the degree he has con-trol over us.

We've got to read God's word and pray, ask God to help us focus our minds on what is good and pure. (Psalm 139:23) Study and think about God's words continually (1 Timothy 4:13-15; Joshua 1:8; Psalm 119:11), and let his thoughts fill your mind.

The tongue

'Birds are entangled by their feet, and people by their tongues; The tongue talks at the head's cost; He who says what he likes shall hear what he does not like; let not thy tongue run away with thy brains; better the foot slip than the tongue; words have wings, and cannot be called back; words bind men; the tongue breaks bone and herself has none; the tongue stings; the tongue is not steel yet it cuts; words cut more than the sword; words are but wind, but blows unkind; a tongue is more venomous than the serpent's stings; a good tongue is a good weapon'.

We stumble many ways, writes James. (James 3: 2-12) But if anyone is never at fault in what he says, he is a perfect man, able to keep his whole body in check. This is a man who tames his tongue. The tongue expresses the content of the heart. As a great forest can be set on fire by a small spark so can the tongue degrade the whole body! It corrupts the whole person, sets the whole course of his life on fire. It is a restless evil and full of deadly poison. We are entangled by our tongue. Under the tongue men are crushed to death. There is no venom to that of the tongue.

Think about this, 'dreams live or die in our months'. As God created the world with words, we can either create or kill with words, with little effort. All that it takes are kind or hash words. A dreamer kills his dream in his own mouth if he does not realise that the ability to control his tongue is a clear mark of wisdom; that his tongue has the power of life and death. The words we use and the thoughts and attitudes behind them determine our future.

We must commit ourselves wholeheartedly to talk about God's promises and our dreams on a continual basis. We must try to help others and build them up with what we say. (Job 16:5; Ephesians 4:29) Giving good advice, when the right time comes (Proverbs 25:11) and speaks words of thanks and praise to one another and to God. (Psalm 50:23)

The eyes

Keep your mouth shut and your eyes open. Some succeed, others fail. Perhaps one reason is that successful people's eyes see where failures can't. To write history, you must see the future, the present as it can be, opportunities, hope in hopelessness and destiny in despair. We must see differently and beyond the facts. We need to see the future for our community, business, family etc so that we can be able to deal with the challenges we face now. Just as Jesus endured the cross and its scorning shame, the humiliation of its suffering because, as runners concentrate on the finishing line, he focused on prospects of future glory, so we also should concentrate on the goal and objective of our purpose in life. We must watch what we watch, otherwise our minds shall be full of rubbish and Satan may have us in bits. There is such rubbish about most television programmes that it's advisable to turn off or switch programmes if it gets bad.

6

THE PILLARS OF LIFE

Standing at the centre of the Quwwatul Mosque the Iron Pillar is one of Delhi's most curious structures. Dating back to 4th century AD, the pillar bears an inscription which states that it was erected as a flagstaff in honour of the Hindu god, Vishnu, and in the memory of the Gupta King Chandragupta II (375-413). How the pillar moved to its present location remains a mystery. The pillar also highlights ancient India's achievements in metallurgy. The pillar is made of 98 per cent wrought iron and has stood 1,600 years without rusting or decomposing.

In the same vein, the Pillars of Hercules appear as supporters of the coat of arms of Spain, originating from the famous _impresa_ of the Holy Roman Emperor, Charles V, who was King of

Spain in the years following the discovery of the Americas. It bears the motto Plus Ultra (Latin for further beyond), encouraging him to ignore the ancient warning, to take risks and go further beyond. It indicates the desire to see the Pillars as an entrance to the rest of the world rather than as a gate to the Mediterranean Sea. It also indicates the overseas possessions that Spain had.

'I have but one lamp by which my feet are guided, and that is the lamp of experience', writes Patrick Henry. I have learnt long ago that life has pillars that are essential in life and a prerequisite to success: positive emotions, wisdom, hope, happiness, love, persistence, character, confidence, discipline, vision, respect, advice and strength.

The seven major negative emotions to be avoided

In Japan great importance is attached to controlling the expression of negative feelings so they are often masked by the Japanese with a smile. This does not mean that Japanese people do not experience feelings of sadness, fear or disgust, but because they are taught that it is impolite to show these feelings in public they do not, while in private they express these emotions.

Emotion is a term used to describe the feeling or experience of being happy, sad, angry or frightened. Emotions arise from a thought or a set of thoughts. Our thoughts about a particular challenge can produce many emotions, for example, excitement, confidence, hope, anxiety, fear, dejection or depression. Negative thinking produces negative emotions: worry, fear, anxiety, stress, rejection and depression; whereas positive thinking produces positive emotions: excitement, confidence and hope.

There are seven major negative emotions that should be avoided if we desire progress and fulfilment:

- Fear
- Jealousy
- Hatred
- Revenge
- Greed
- Superstition
- Anger

Negative emotions hinder dreams, cripple growth and stunt future progress. They build doubt rather than faith in God. God has good and perfect plans for us. He wants us to be transformed people with renewed minds – people of faith that can see possibilities and look forward to the future. More than the people of Japan, we must 'cut off the head of negative emotions' with the Word of God, prayer and the help of the Holy Spirit.

The seven major positive emotions to develop

Jane and Emma are writing their GSCE examination today. Jane has prepared well for the examination and therefore thinks of the examination as a challenge. Emma has done little preparation and thinks of the examination as a threat. As they go into the examination hall, Jane is full of excitement, confidence and hope whereas Emma is worried, anxious and fearful.

Janet and Emma's emotions arise from their thoughts to do with the examination and their level of preparation. Their emotions will eventually affect the way their body functions both internally and externally. For example, Emma may feel 'butterflies in her stomach' because of her anxiety. Her heart will beat faster and her skin will perspire more than normal. Muscular activity in the arms, legs and trunk will alter, but the most important type of visible change will be in her facial expression. Happiness, sadness, surprise, disgust, fear and anger are expressed in the face in distinctive and easily recognised ways.

There are seven powerful positive emotions which should dominate our minds to catapult us to a higher level in life. These are:

- Desire
- Faith
- Love

Michael Marnu

- Sex
- Enthusiasm
- Romance
- Hope.

What we put into our minds determines what comes out in our words and actions. Programme the minds with thoughts that are true, noble, right, pure, lovely, admirable, excellent and praiseworthy (Philippians 4:8). Replace harmful input with wholesome material. With diligent Bible study, prayer and practice in focusing the mind on what is good and pure, we can develop positive emotions.

Hold fast to the hope in your heart and hang on there

There have been times I have basket full of bills to pay, letters from debt collectors, repossession orders and many more but I always do my best to view such problems as challenges and to never lose hope. The very first day my property was to be repossessed, at the Magistrates' Court, I thought of Gemma Quinn who was paralysed from the neck down after breaking her neck in a car accident. Despite being told she would have to spend the rest of her life on a ventilator she amazed doctors by returning to school, taking her GSCE examinations and raising £100,000 for spinal research. Gemma hit the headlines in 1995 after she wrote a letter to Christopher Reeve urging him not to give up hope when he was paralysed in a show-jumping accident.

Reeve was inspired by Gemma's words at a time when he was at his lowest ebb. Her stated goal was to raise enough money to fund a cure for paralysis by the time she turned 21. Think about this, she who must be pitied gave hope to the suffering. What about me?

It is easy to become preoccupied with troubles that confront us daily. Some of these difficulties may appear insurmountable. In reality, we have plenty of reasons to be hopeful about life. No matter how hopeless life may seem at the moment, we have reason for hope on earth. Hope should be the last thing we abandon. Let death alone kill our hope for hope will keep us alive. People who lose hope of some sort or another usually become an enemy of society, lash out or drop out.

The need for hope can be compared to the 206 bones of human beings. These bones form the supporting and protective framework for the whole body. Just as bones have to be strong in proportion to the size of the body it supports, so does the level of hope in a person. The level of hope in our life determines our ability and strength to go on.

Whatever the affliction, there is total deliverance out of every adversity. God will use our circumstances to show His strength.

The holy grail of happiness is within your reach

I have also learnt that one of the most powerful forces in the world is happiness. There is a correlation between unhappiness and criminality; happiness and responsible behaviour. Happy people are rarely wicked; the majority of criminals come from unhappy homes and have a history of broken relationships. We think better, perform better, feel better and are healthier when we are happy. When thinking pleasant thoughts, we can see, taste and hear better. Our memory is greatly improved as our mind is relaxed.

No one can be happy 100 per cent of the time. However, happiness is produced, not by objects, but by our trust in God and ability to manage our ideas, thoughts and attitudes, irrespective of our circumstances. Happiness shouldn't be made contingent upon solving external problems because when one problem is solved, another appears in its place.

There are three keys to happiness. It starts off with contentment. Contentment is a rare bird that sings sweetly in the breast. Discontentment makes rich men poor. We must avoid self-pity. It turns molehills into mountains. We must always look at the positives in life. Every day is a mixture of good and evil. It is merely a matter of what we choose to give our primary attention to and what thoughts we have in our own minds.

To turn minuses into pluses requires wisdom

'I am a practical man. Much of my experiences have been based on common sense. I hereby advise you to get wisdom, discipline and understanding' (Proverbs 23:23). A wise man never wants a weapon.

A crisis arose in the early church. The conflict between the Jewish believers and the new Gentile believers threatened to divide the church. They gathered to consider this matter. After much debate James said, 'For it seemed good ... to lay upon you no greater burden than the necessary things ...' words of wisdom resolved the budding conflict.

To turn minuses into pluses in life requires wisdom. Wisdom gives balance and helps to avoid eccentricity and extravagance. We need wisdom to see difficulties in their true light and to profit from them. Difficulties often overwhelm us; create struggles that require resolution. Wisdom is more than wide-reaching knowledge; it is the ability to discern, which enables us to meet life and its difficulties with decision and action. Wisdom is a queenly regulative discretion that sees and selects worthy ends and the best means of attaining them. It is a combination of discernment, judgment and sagacity. If knowledge is the accumulation of facts and intelligence the development of reason, wisdom is discernment: insight into the heart of things. More than knowledge, wisdom demands the correct application of knowledge to a matter, such as handling dilemmas correctly or negotiating complex relationships effectively. Wisdom is nine-tenths a matter of being wise at the time. Doing the right thing at the right time is at the heart of wisdom. Unfortunately many people are too often wise after the event.

If you feel unable to look at your difficulties, seek insight and wisdom from God (James 1:5) and you will grow stronger and wiser. He is the source of true wisdom.

Love rules his kingdom without a sword

I have learnt this over and over again throughout my life. 'Love rules his kingdom without a sword.' No doubt. Cupid, the Roman god of love was represented as a blindfolded child epitomising the real meaning of love: 'Love is blind'. Love is blind because it sees no fault; in the eyes of the lover, pockmarks are dimples. Love is lawless and is without reason. One cannot love and be wise at the same time. It is said that affection blinds reason and lovers are always mad, 'because love covers over a multitude of sins'. (1 Peter 4:8). Faults are thick where love is thin. Where love fails, we espy all faults. Undoubtedly, love is the touchstone of virtue and the summary of God's Ten Commandments. Jesus' key to life was love. He taught us to love one another. Love was His golden rule.

Love is a powerful tool of life. It conquers all. It is as strong as death. It finds a way to go through stone walls. In love there is no lack. It shows in times of need and casts out fear. (1 John 4:18) It makes the world go around and makes all men people equal. It makes all hard hearts gentle and speaks when the lips are closed.

Obviously, it is not advisable to rely on love. It may be sweet in the beginning but sour at the end. The course of love never runs smooth. But true love never grows old. Sound love is not soon forgotten and it never goes rusty. Lovers may quarrel, yet such quarrels are soon mended; a lovers' quarrel is a renewal of their love. 'I now am giving you a new commandment; Love each other; just as I have loved you ... Your love for one another will prove to the world that you are my disciples.' (John 13:34-35) God has made us together. He expects us to love and to live in peace with others.

Compassion
An event was unfolded when Dion went to pick up a friend from work in New Cross, London. A young man was on the ground nearby gasping for breath. Hardly had Dion thought that she would provide comfort to a young man who had been shot. Having called the police she went to the aid of the victim, talking to him and encouraging him to remain calm. She felt blessed that she was there to help. This event has changed her life for good.

According to the Oxford Dictionary, compassion is a feeling or emotion when a person is moved by the suffering or distress of another, and by a desire to relieve it. Compassion comes to the aid of those needing help, either physically or spiritually. When Jesus upheld the legal penalty for adultery – stoning the woman caught in adultery (John 8:7) – he highlighted the importance of compassion and forgiveness.

When others have sinned we should not be quick to pass judgment. To judge others is to act as though we have never sinned. It is God's role to judge, not ours; our role is to show forgiveness and compassion. Learn not to take advantage of people during their time of extreme need. Always go beyond simply keeping the law and show compassion. Show personal care so as not to hurt other people. Express genuine concern for others, but at the same time be always ready to accept advice from others as much as offer your support.

When people are going through severe trials, ill-advised counsel is distasteful; they may listen politely while inside they are upset. (Job 6:6-7)

We can show compassion if we learn to develop humility, contentment, empathy and love. A humble person does not feel above those in need of help. Contentment keeps us from being too busy to help the needy. To the extent that we are able to put ourselves in another's shoes, we will be able to show compassion. Generous, principled love will help us manifest compassion. Wherever we live there are needy people close by and there is no good reason for refusing to help them.

Return evil for evil to no man

A good heart conquers ill-fortune. Watch Tower magazine recently cited a New York Times article from 18 March 1968 which reported, 'Bound youth burned to death: 19 Seized', telling of the way in which one motorcycle gang wreaked vengeance on the leader of a rival gang, being an instance of the many injustices carried out, and injury or harm done to others, as an act of vengeance. It is tempting to react hastily according to our feelings and knowledge. We may go to war, go out on strike, make a protest, start a riot, demonstrate and retaliate for actual or alleged maltreatment. We are faced with a decision as to how we will react and what course of action we will take.

There are many events about which we hear or experience that cause indignation, but as Christians our reaction should be worthy. Jesus Christ suggested a radical response to injustice: (Matthew 5:43-47) 'turn the other cheek'. Retaliation is not our weapon, for it is more important to give justice and mercy than to receive it. Instead of demanding rights, we must give them up freely. We must not take the law into our own hands. By loving and praying for our enemies we can overcome the evil with the good. Do not love only those who love in return and feel hatred for your enemies.

Conquering the evil with the good shows that Jesus is Lord of our life and that we have given ourselves fully to God, because only He can deliver us from selfishness. Turning the other cheek requires mature thinking, self-control and long-suffering, all of which is possible with the help of the Holy Spirit.

The beauty of mercy
We need to offer mercy to each other and be willing to receive it from each other. God says, 'When your partner offends you, you should forgive and comfort one another, so you won't give up in despair.' (2 Corinthians 2:7) In truth, society needs mercy to lubricate the friction generated in everyday life. An integral part of 'peace on earth' is mercy. Mercy is more kindness than justice requires: it is kindness beyond what can be claimed or expected. Kind treatment or pity surpasses justice. Mercilessness locks the door of forgiveness and opens up the door of hatred; its demands are beyond that which we should demand of others.

There is no relationship without mercy. God warns, 'Never hold grudges' (Colossians 3:13) because bitterness and resentment always destroy fellowship. Because we are imperfect, sinful people we inevitably hurt one another when we are together for long enough.

Sometimes we hurt each other intentionally and sometimes unintentionally, but either way, it takes enormous amounts of mercy and grace to create and maintain the relationship. We should make allowances for each other's faults and forgive those who offend us. Pardons and pleasantness are great revenge for slanderous deeds. Mercilessness causes many of the world's troubles and conflicts; billions of innocent lives are shattered with merciless attitudes. Without mercy we see marriages breaking down and relationships, generally, impossible to maintain. He who forgives gains the victory, so wink at small faults.

The power of kindness

'A kind man benefits himself but a cruel man brings trouble on himself.' (Proverbs 11:17) When you continue to love your enemies, do good works and lend without interest, not hoping for anything back – this is what kindness is all about. Contrarily, in the world today, acts of kindness are often done in the hope of some benefit; done in some selfish way that hopes for something back or some favour in return. Often kindness is seen as some sort of 'bribe'; some may take offence if their kindness receives nothing back.

I have learnt to do good works without hoping for anything back. I am ready to do good things for all men, try to be merciful, compassionate, benevolent, patient, friendly, hospitable, generous, considerate, gentle and obliging. My loving kindness, I firmly believe, is the fruit of the in-dwelling Holy Spirit. It is a proof of the presence of the Holy Spirit because it is only the Spirit of God that can transform us to put-off selfishness.

True kindness is powerful and has the ability to inspire us to do what is right in all affairs of life. It is expressed both in language and in deeds. It aids us in being tactful, polite, and courteous; to pursue peace and to maintain harmony. It puts misunderstanding to flight and clears the way for forgiveness. Loving kindness solves problems and attracts more kindness, repelling unkindness. If we are true to our faith and pursue goodness, compassion and kindness without motive, our reward will be great and we shall be the sons of the Most High God. (Ephesians 5:1; Luke 6:35) In truth a kind heart loseth nought at last.

The world demands a standard of character from you

'A good name is better than fine perfume. He is wise that is honest.' A time will come when our lifestyles will be scrutinised; when our faults will run around on two little legs. There was a story about a young and promising politician in the United Kingdom. He was a colourful millionaire peer, a trusted friend of the prime minister. The prime minister made him deputy chairman of the party and gave him a peerage; he was praised to the heavens. His career was crushed, however, when he contested for a mayoral seat; his lifestyle put under scrutiny as a consequence, he was tried and sentenced to prison.

While we should be open to criticism, people should respect us fundamentally for our high ideals of character. Ensure that detractors have not a rung to stand on by ensuring that there are no grounds for reproach or indictment of wrongdoing. Our adversaries should find no opening for a smear campaign, rumour mongering or gossip; our character should command the respect of the world, inspire confidence and arouse aspiration. Strive to be above reproach and of unchallengeable morality. Do not allow a secret indulgence that would undermine public witness: command respect! Be genial and gentle, not a lover of controversy. Solve a problem rather than pick a fight and always remember good rather than evil; the good we receive rather than the good we have done. Do not be covetous and a lover of money.

No one is born with godly character. It is developed through experience, trials, adversities and a commitment to know God and His Word. (Deuteronomy 8:2) I have been there before. This foundation determines what the fate of your assassins will be.

Let your 'Yes' be 'Yes'

'Do not lie to each other, for you have stripped off your old nature ...' (Colossians 3:9) We must let our 'yes' be 'yes' and 'no' be 'no'.

In the summer of 2009 it was reported that a Ministry of Defence press officer was suing his bosses having suffered post-traumatic stress disorder as a result of having to 'peddle lies' about the war in Basaq. He claimed he had to 'defend the morally indefensible' when telling newspapers that army vehicles could withstand roadside bombs. He said the pain of visiting more than a dozen families devastated by the loss of their relatives in war zones also shattered him. He was particularly plagued by the thought that some of the bereaved families he was visiting might have previously believed their loved ones were safe because of what he himself had said to the media.

Making claims that you can't substantiate and embellishing statements with superlatives are endemic in the modern world. Why do we need to swear in everyday conversation? Is it that we are so insecure that we need to strengthen our words with bold claims? Rabbi Shmuley Boteach believes that if you are confident that what you are saying will be accepted, there is no need to swear. He counsels us, therefore, to be as good as our word and not to 'stretch the truth'. Avoid making false commitments that you do not intend to fulfil. Do not make promises that you never intend to keep. Be careful not to get carried away with excitement and make outrageous claims or make promises that are clearly beyond your ability.

On the other side of the coin, it is tempting to exaggerate the truth about ourselves. Many people feel inadequate and insecure so try to impress others by inflating the importance of their jobs and attributes. The tragedy is that 'stretching the truth' about ourselves and our prowess will never work in the long term; sooner or later the truth will be out. Be confident in yourself.

God hates deception and lying. (Psalm 5:6; Proverbs 6:16-19; Isaiah 59:2-3; Zephaniah 3:13) He has commanded us not to lie. Christ never lied. Those who practise deceit face eternal judgment in hell. (Revelation 21:27)

Respect

The man who becomes a great leader usually has respect for his followers that is as deep and real as their respect for him, writes Rich DeVos. According to Rich DeVos it is not love that makes the world go round. In practical terms, in our day-to-day contact with people, respect is what makes the world go round. No doubt the word of God entreats us to 'Love each one with genuine affection, and take delight in honouring each other'. (Romans 12:10)

The ancient Greek philosophers, Plato and Aristotle, wrestled with notions of freedom and justice in ancient Greek society, just as Britain, much later looked to the Magna Carta and English Bill of Rights (1688-9). The adoption of the Universal Declaration of Human Rights (1948), The European Convention for the Protection of Human Rights (1950) and the founding of Amnesty International in 1961 were institutional efforts to entrench respect for human rights in all societies. Although the protection of human rights is top of the agenda in many countries today, human rights may be all the more effective if each and every one of us lay it upon himself to love and serve his neighbour; fought for his neighbour's rights, while being ready to renounce his own.

The way to show respect for another person is by being sincere and honest in all our dealings with them. Never underestimate the power of honesty to attract other people. After all, one of the hardest things to do in life is to resist the urge to get ahead even if it means we have to cheat a little. Show no partiality in your attitude to other people, and give no special deference to some because they are rich, famous or influential. Neither defer to the rich and powerful, nor despise the poor and the weak, but give equal respect to all, whatever their social status. For human rights are equal rights.

If sometimes you look down on people remember 'Just as water reflects the face, so one human heart reflects another. What you show people will be reflected back. Use them and they will end up using you. Respect them and they will respect you.'

A soft answer turns away wrath

Over the years, I have learned that the tongue is a small part of the body, but it makes great boast ... ' (James 3:4-6). A wise king said, 'A soft answer turns away wrath, but grievous words stir up anger ... The tongue of the wise utters knowledge rightly, but the mouth of the fool pours out folly ... A soft speech breaks down the most bone-like resistance'. Both words of blessing and wicked words are very powerful. (Proverbs 11:11; Proverbs 15:1) It is always hard to argue with someone who insists on answering gently. Contrarily, a raised voice and harsh words almost always trigger an angry response. Gideon calmed the anger of the men of Ephraim with a gentle answer. (Judges 8: 1-3) Nabal's sarcastic response put David in a fighting mood. (1 Samuel 25: 10-13) A good tongue is a good weapon.

Tact and diplomacy are like two sides of a coin. Tact is the ability to deal with people sensitively, to avoid giving offence, to have a feel for the proper words or response to a delicate situation. Diplomacy, on the other hand, is the ability to manage delicate situations, especially involving people from different cultures and certainly those with differing opinions. For peace among men to be a reality we need to reconcile opposing viewpoints without giving offence or compromising principles. We must

Michael Marnu

own empathy, the ability to project into the life, heart and mind of another. We must set aside personal preferences and deal with the other in a fashion that fits the other best. We must come to a point in our life of being able to negotiate differences in a way that recognises mutual rights and intelligence and yet reach a harmonious solution.

If you find it difficult to give a soft answer, remember that the key to tact and diplomacy lies in an understanding of how people feel and react. The tongue must be bridled. (James 3:4-6)

Advice
One of the biggest lessons I have learnt in life had to do with advice.The Holy Scriptures command us to go to the ant ... consider its ways and be wise' (Proverbs 6:6). It's safer to hear and take counsel, than to give it. A wise man will hear and increase learning'. (Proverbs 1:5)

Evil kings of the Old Testament did not like God's prophets bringing messages of doom. Many, therefore, hired prophets who told them only what they wanted to hear. These men extolled the greatness of the kings and predicted victory, regardless of the real situation. This is insanity.

Good counsel has no price and it never comes too late. Good counsel provides valuable information, gives direction, warns about the ills of the future and imparts knowledge to make us more experienced and wise. Wisdom makes us more prosperous and keeps us from stumbling. He that will not be counselled cannot be helped. Counsel must, however, be followed and not simply praised. 'In vain he craves advice that will not follow it.'

Counsel can be given by the wise: the healthy gives counsel to the sick. It is said that if you wish for good advice, consult an old man, just as it is said 'night is the mother of counsel'. There are many sayings promoting good counsel: 'the best advice is found on the pillow'; 'who knows a fool may give a wise man counsel so as an enemy, a woman and your own soul' and 'if the counsel is good, no matter who gave it'.

What you listen to and from who are crucial, so be selective and remember, too much consulting confounds for it fogs the situation. It is also said 'Steer not after every mariner's direction' and 'he that spears all opinions comes with ill speed'. Take counsel soberly; keep your own good judgement: 'the worst counsel is that given in wine for it seldom prospers.' In the Psalms (1:1) it is said that bad communication also ruins good life. We are told that 'Ill counsel mars all' and that 'the land is never void of counsellors. Nothing is given so freely as advice.' Advice comes in many guises: 'Advice is a stranger; if welcome he stays for the night; if not welcome he returns home the same day.'

Then we are warned about waiting until it is too late: 'when a thing is done, advice comes too late'. Most importantly, heed this advice: 'the first degree of folly is to hold one's self wise, the second to profess it, and the third to despise counsel.'

The young grow weak

I also believe that, 'he does not receive the victor's crown unless he competes according to the rules'. (2 Timothy 2:5) 'Even those who are young grow weak, young people can fall exhausted'. Every vision has a tendency to fade. Every visionary is prone to discouragement. Hard work that began with zeal can easily degenerate into drudgery as suffering and loneliness take their toll. Even the leader feels neglected and gets tired. It takes discipline to master passion; time and energy to grow it and finish the race. Before we can the get best out of life, self-discipline is essential, for without this quality, writes J. Oswald Sanders; all other gifts remain dwarfed and cannot grow.

We are on the road to success when we learn to obey discipline imposed from 'without' and take on a more rigorous discipline from within. Those who rebel against authority and scorn self-discipline seldom become winners.

Many who remain mediocre are sufficiently worthy for much more in human standards, but with large areas of their life floating free, they are out of control. Lazy and disorganised, they never achieve the best life can offer them. A person who has the desire to get the most out of life will work diligently while others only waste time, and will study while others snooze, notes Oswald Sanders. Slothful habits can be overcome, whether in thought or in deed. The winning spirit without reluctance will undertake the unpleasant task that others avoid, or the hidden duty that others evade, even if it wins no public applause. Never known to procrastinate, he will prefer to dispatch the hardest tasks first.

Self-discipline involves first knowing God's guidelines for right living. Regular, consistent reading of God's Word keeps His guidelines for right living clearly before us. He that is master of himself will soon be master of others

The ability to deal with impossible situations is the key to success

I am very optimistic as ever that God will give me every place where I set my foot ...' (Joshua 1:3). Sir Cliff Richard's music has been banned by many radio stations, yet he has sold millions of records. A tabloid newspaper has acknowledged that due to the attitude of the radio stations, 'it's a miracle Cliff sells any records at all!' The Sun for example wrote, 'Everyone hates him. So how come Cliff is number 2 in the charts. He has sold more single records in Britain than anyone else – including Elvis and the Beatles – and is the only pop star ever to notch up a No. 1 in every decade since the fifties.'

Have you come to the 'Red Sea' impasse in your life, where in spite of all you can do, there is no way out, no way back? There is no other way but through a place J. Oswald Sanders names the 'Impossible Situation'. There is one ingredient found often in people of valour but missing in many other people, this is the ability to deal with impossible tasks rather than easy ones. Until we start to handle our problems we cannot foster personal competence, teamwork and confidence. If we cease to occupy ourselves with minor things, which could be done by others, we can reach new heights. Think about this: 'A man who is on the verge of success always rises to face baffling circumstances and complex problems'. We have abilities to match every impossible situation whose power gets ignited when we face the situation. At times when we meet the impossible our strategies sound like fantasy. The reality is that it is a defining moment of our destiny.

The world is full of difficult problems and adverse circumstances. To survive as successful and mature human beings we must view the difficult as commonplace and the complex as normal. Plug into your source of strength: Jehovah through Jesus Christ. He has promised to give us every place where we set our feet ... (Joshua 1:3). Without danger we cannot get beyond danger

People who use their talents to the maximum are more fulfilled

I have been blessed by God to be fruitful'. (Genesis 1:28) There are no spare parts in humans. I have been hand-picked and placed on this earth for a special purpose. I have a definite part to play. My role is suited to my gifts, talents, abilities, weaknesses and personality. I have therefore resolved to take the once-in-a lifetime initiative, to make and keep a simple heartfelt goal or commitment and record it for life. Everything counts. Singly or together I must make a positive difference. God sees me as a person by whom and through whom He can do great works. He sees me as already serene, confident and cheerful. He sees me not as a pathetic victim of life, but as a master in the art of living, not seeking sympathy but imparting help to others.

My reasoning, creativity, speech, self-determination and character – my entire self – reflects the image of God. Knowing that I am made in God's image and thus share many of His characteristics provides a solid basis my self-worth. I know God is the all wise, all-powerful and all-knowing creator, and made in His likeness, I would not turn out to be an inferior product. My self-worth is not based on possessions, achievements, physical attractions or public acclaim, but on being made in God's image. For this reason, I feel positive about myself.

The Nigerians have a saying, 'A hunter who has only one arrow does not shoot with careless aim.' Unlike the cat, which is thought by some to have nine lives, we humans have only one life, the significance of which should be self-evident. It is somewhat disheartening that many people waste their lives, impeded by frustration, emptiness, disgust, hopelessness, apathy and anger. They don't believe in themselves and always expect the worst for themselves. They are always worried about how they look, what others will think of them or whether they are going to fail in life. Think about this, we live in a significant period of time. People are becoming conscious of themselves as a powerful thinking individual with the capabilities to achieve anything they set their mind on.

'I always press on towards the goal to win the prize for which God has called me in Christ Jesus.' The Apostle Paul says that his goal is to know Christ, and to be all Christ has in mind for him. (Philippians 3:14) This goal absorbs all his energy. This is a helpful example for me. I do not let anything take my eyes off my goal in life. With the single mindedness of an athlete in training, I always lay aside everything harmful and forsake anything that may distract me from being an effective person.

Dieter Wiesner, who managed the late Michael Jackson from 1996 to 2003, claimed 'Jacko' cried in private because he believed no one loved him; he also lived in fear that social services would swoop on him. Wiesner claimed that Jackson plunged deeper into drug addiction in the wake of Martin Bashir's 2003 TV documentary. It broke him. It killed him. He took a long time to die, but it started that night.

Many people spend their time avoiding responsibility by 'passing the buck' rather than tackling challenges head on. They turn their back on responsibility because it is a lot easier to avoid it than deal with it. Accepting responsibility is a choice but accepting responsibility for your life is what separates the adults from the children. Burke Hedges writes, 'You and only you are responsible for your life ... the only person who can add value to your life is you ...' Assuming responsibility for whom and what you are puts you on the road to success. People who exercise their talents to the maximum are more fulfilled and purposeful and have the ability to make things happen.

Life is concerned with obtaining practical results from different situations. Without exception, the effective person is more aware of their responsibilities than of personal perks and benefits; they get great satisfaction from achieving the impossible. In view of this, the achievers confront and overcome demanding situations. We can acknowledge that we are not responsible for what happens to us, but we must also accept that we are responsible for the way we respond to what happens to us. It is not so much what happens to us but what we do with it that matters. Fruitfulness is ingrained in all of us by God but it comes after hard work. Remember Jesus' parable of the talents and that the worthless servant was thrown into darkness where there was weeping and gnashing of teeth. (Matthew 25:14-30) Every man is the architect of his own fortune.

Sow tears and reap joy!

I believe in hard work. I choose to work hard and become a leader rather than be lazy and become a slave'. (Proverbs 12:24) The secret of genius is drudgery. For Thomas Edison, genius was 'one per cent inspiration and 99 per cent perspiration', for Thomas Carlyle genius was 'the transcendent capacity of taking trouble'. Hard work is the hallmark of history's successful people. Read the biographies and autobiographies of successful people and you discover that they all added hard work to their visions. Thomas Edison made 1000 experiments before he invented the electric light bulb.

Winston Churchill loathed the Nazi tyranny and dreamt of European liberation but was under no illusion about the cost of the enterprise. On 13 May 1940, in his first speech to the House of Commons as prime minister, he warned members that he had nothing to offer but blood, toil, tears and sweat and many long months of struggling and suffering. Ghana's first prime minister and president, Kwame Nkrumah, worked up political slogans that praised toil, such as 'Work and Happiness'.

A thriving life prioritises growth and pays the price for it. It thinks: 'I have a dream to which I shall commit, for my commitment shall determine how far I shall go. In view of this, I shall invest my blood, sweat and tears to pursue my dream to excellence. This is a dream for my own life, and I am not working for anybody else ...' Success does not happen by chance, it comes about by setting primary goals and then planning and programming to meet those goals. Every goal is a statement of faith. 'Work hard and become a leader; be lazy and become a slave.' (Proverbs 12:24)

Be careful what you think

By far the most vital lesson I have ever learnt is the importance of what I think. If I know what you think, I would know what you are. Our thoughts make us what we are'. The 19th-century poet and essayist, Ralph Waldo Emerson, believed that 'A man is what he thinks about all day long.' The biggest challenge to living a full and useful life lies in your thoughts; with the right mindset we are on the road to success. With the right 'inner dialogue' every circumstance is seen as an opportunity to develop the character.

Negative assumptions about life produce bad feelings, which in turn produce bad behaviour. If we think happy thoughts, we will be happy. If we wallow in self-pity everyone will want to shun us. Life is what our thoughts make it. Assuming a positive attitude instead of a negative one;

being optimistic rather than being pessimistic is an indispensable trait of successful people. A positive mindset makes everything possible, you produce more, achieving maximum effectiveness, and favourable results inevitably follow. In truth, it is not the circumstances in which we find ourselves that is important, it is the thoughts we attach to these circumstances that drive the outcome. He who conquers his mind is mightier than he who takes a city. As the 17th-century English poet, John Milton, noted the mind can make a heaven out of hell and hell out of heaven. It is for this reason that Epiletus warned us to be more concerned about removing wrong thoughts from the mind than removing tumours and abscesses from the body.

Possibility thinking

Pastor Robert Schuller of Crystal Cathedral has experienced a growth rate of over 500 per cent in a decade. Crystal Cathedral's membership of 10,000 is evidence of 'possibility thinking'. The miracle happened when Pastor Schuller fixed his attention on a slogan written across the top of his wall calendar: 'I'd rather attempt to do something great and fail than attempt to do nothing and succeed'.

Possibility thinking is 'the maximum utilisation of God-given powers of imagination exercised in dreaming up possible ways by which a desired objective can be attained'. If you have a dream, you need only to exercise this miracle-working power and you can reach seemingly unattainable goals. 'If you have a faith as a mustard seed ... ' (Matthew 17:20) nothing can keep you from growing or achieving whatever you want. Possibility thinking looks ahead by faith and visualises making it, affirming that in all probability you will do well. Remember, if we fail to plan we plan to fail, so possibility thinking relies on faith and involves setting goals; but planning and programming to meet those goals is critical.

Moving forward is a venture into the unknown; there is risk involved and there are sure to be stumbles and mistakes but do not be afraid. The most formidable obstacle to success is negative thinking. The power we receive in union with Christ is sufficient to do His will and to face the challenges that arise from our commitment to doing it. As we face challenges, troubles and pressures, we ask Christ to strengthen us.

Stinking thinking

Think about waves that disturb the surface of water causing motion, turning the surface of the water into a series of ridges and troughs. Each ridge moves along the surface of the water, not advancing at any great rate: waves, constantly rolling in and out, are restless because they are subject to the forces of wind, gravity and tide times. Doubt leaves people as unsettled as the restless waves.

Many people are living with frustration; captives of the doubt it creates and placing a negative mind lid on their potential. An optimistic attitude is not a luxury; it is a necessity. The biggest problem is our thoughts; it is our thoughts that help or hinder us in making the best out of life. With the right mindset we are on the road to success. God made us big on the inside but life can make us feel small. Nevertheless, within us is the power to turn every situation around. Change your thinking. Big dreams come from big thinkers.

Stinking thinking hinders dreams. It cripples growth and stunts future progress. Getting motivated is very difficult when an inner voice constantly insists that 'it can't be done'. For every opportunity you will find someone with an excuse. Excuses confirm doubt rather than faith. Success is not built on the negative voices of doubt but on the positive foundations of faith. Doubt is cumulative, and causes friction and division; negative thinking promotes a mentality of under-achievement. Stinking thinking lacks purpose or joy; it is damaging emotionally and causes misery and ill-health, pulling you down instead of building you up. Stinking-thinking people often find fault with others, focusing on their worst, rather than their best aspects. Stinking thinking does not help you solve a problem; on the contrary, it creates boundaries and limits achievement.

Life is what our thoughts make it and, as the English poet, John Milton, observed, 'The mind can make a heaven out of hell and hell out of heaven'.

The win–lose mentality

When I read the story 'Jones let his people down' I laughed but I learned a lesson from it. Selfishness was ingrained in the mind of this particular individual, Jones, who had achieved some form of success, and was supposed to be responsible for helping his people to achieve a better standard of life. Instead, he created a 'Buppie' class, which looked down on the people, aiding them in a condescending manner. His selfishness did not allow him to work with others on a project or endeavour. He steadfastly refused to see that working together achieves more than working alone. He did not understand that he was no better than others despite what he owned.

The win–lose mentality ('scarcity' or 'survival of the fittest' mentality) describes people who are covetous and selfish. They believe that the world has limited resources, so that anything that others have deprives them of their rightful share. Blind to God's infinite and unlimited supply of good things, they do not realise that no one has to lose in order for them to win. As one candle can light 10,000 others without losing its intensity so we have been made in God's image, together. To live is to be part of a fellowship or a relationship and to support it loyally. Our sense of pride should not depend on our ability to outdo others. Our glory is best defined when everyone involved in the achievement shares in it equally.

God has a perfect plan for everybody. We must believe in God's providence and be satisfied with what we have. We must appreciate and accept that what we have is a blessing from God, thereby leaving no room to covet anything that belongs to another man. Covetousness is forever filling a bottomless vessel and is the root of all evil, breaking the sack and starving other vices. The covetous person grabs everything but brings nothing home. Remember, 'It is not the man who has little, but he who desires more, that is poor.' In always thinking win-win, the world will become a better place.

The victory mentality
What ultimately motivates my friends is often my victory mentality. I have been described as a great motivator, and friends seeks my moral support in their ventures.

Victory mentality exists above and beyond challenges and troubles to pursue its goal, irrespective of circumstances or limitations. Refusing to remain a victim of circumstances, he that owns the victory mentality does not entertain resentment or frustration and becomes stronger and better rather than bitter. He knows that feeling sorry for oneself is not only a waste of energy but is also a waste of time. Regardless of circumstances, he stands firm, strong, mighty and invincible and has decided not to be discouraged by life.

Where I have been in life is not what matters, it is where I am going that is important. Everybody gets hurt, and nobody escapes disappointments, loss, pain and suffering. All of us will face negative experiences, which sometimes prompt us to change our attitudes and lifestyle. Hurt is hurt and failure is failure, no matter how it is packaged, but your responses to these episodes makes all the difference. We can choose to master these problems rather than let them control our lives.

If our trust is fully in the God of hope, our life shall abound in hope. I have deep faith and trust in the Lord, as the Bible counsels many times: 'Jesus is seated calmly waiting for his enemies to be put under his footstool'; (Romans 16:20) 'all things are working together for good'; (Romans 8:28) 'He will perfect that which concerns us'; (Hebrews 10:14) 'we are to stand still and see the salvation of God. (Exodus 14:13) I am therefore buoyant in life irrespective of troubles.

Within a decision the dream becomes an illusion

I am not afraid to take decisions. When all the facts are known, the ability to make a swift and clear decision is my mark. We may dare to dream, but without a decision, the dream becomes illusion. Many a time, we are quick to declare a preference but lack the courage to weigh evidence and make a decision based on sound judgement.

The essence of life is in decision making: the process by which you choose among various courses of action in order to achieve your goal. Once sure of the vision you must spring into action without regard for the consequences. However, a sincere but faulty decision, writes J. Oswald Sanders, 'is worse than weak-willed trial balloons or indecisive overtones'.

It is easier to make the correct decision when one keeps in mind what one is trying to accomplish. The right decision puts us on the right road to victory. Decisions are made in relation to goals, and are well made if objectives are attained. In most decisions, the key element is not so much knowing what to do, but in living with the results. Yet neither circumstances nor difficulties should deter or frustrate us.

The number-one enemy of decision is procrastination and vacillation. Successful people do not procrastinate when faced with a decision, nor vacillate after making it. To postpone making a decision is really to decide for the status quo. Remember always that, 'the formula for making a decision is like this, I have a vision; I have counted the cost; I have made up my mind; I shall go into action'.

What influences your decisions?

Adam made the wrong decision to eat of the tree's fruit in disobedience of God's command and he polluted the human race. Contrarily, Jesus Christ made the right decision to obey God and changed the history of man's destiny for good. Decisions are an inevitable part of life. Decisions vary from trivial to complex ones, but all decisions impact on our lives and the lives of our loved ones, or even on the entire society. Decisions may also determine the circumstances of the rest of your life.

Decisions are influenced by our own fleshly tendencies of selfishness: fear, pride and jealousy; other people, our peers, parents, pastors, workmates, or our individual circumstance. We are increasingly becoming 'lovers of themselves, lovers of money … lovers of pleasure rather than lovers of God' as Paul prophesied. (2 Timothy 3:2-4) These Godless qualities ourselves and people around us possess have a tendency to influence our decisions.

There are two types of people with whom we may be surrounded, the bad friends who discourage us and trample on our dreams, and the good friends who lift us up and inspire us. 'Stay away from a foolish man, for you will not find knowledge on his lips.' (Proverbs 14:7) 'He who walks with the wise shall be wise.' (Proverbs 13:20) As Watch Tower magazine warns, the influence of unbelievers in the work place, at school or in the neighbourhood; on the radio, television and the newspapers are potent influences in our decision making.

In order to make sound decisions get the facts, be open to new ideas and make sure you hear both sides of the story. God's Word should be influential in your decision making: study it carefully and apply its principles to your circumstances. Talk over your decision with mature and experienced brothers and pastors and seek the influence of God himself through prayer.

Overcoming pressures

A spate of suicides has claimed its 24th victim in just 18 months at the telecommunication giant, France Telecom. The latest employee to kill himself was a father of two who jumped off a bridge onto a motorway. He left a letter for his wife saying the atmosphere at work had driven him to end his life. He was known to have been 'under pressure' having moved from one job dealing with business clients to another at a call centre that made cold calls to offer services to subscribers.

At times we begin projects that seem worthwhile, but something happens to discourage us. That something – call it pressure – can come from within or from an external source. It may be physical or mental exhaustion, a personal challenge or sense of personal failure, or bitter disappointment. A common source of

discouragement can come from negative remarks or criticisms from our relatives, friends,
workmates or employers, which may make us
feel belittled or ridiculed. When we become
discouraged, we suffer a temporary loss of op-
timism, lack courage and hope, and feel 'low of
spirit'. It is, therefore, imperative to overcome
the pressures that lead to discouragement.

A person whose life changes radically may
experience contempt from his old friends. He
may be scorned, not only because he refuses
to participate in certain activities, but also
because his priorities change as he decides
to head in the opposite direction. His life may
incriminate their sinful activity. As we take a
decision to follow a course of action, our values,
morals, goals and purposes will set us apart
from others. We may not neglect them, but
our commitment to our vision must be more
important than those who oppose us; our own
purpose should be the priority. This is the test
of our attitude; how we respond to the often
opposing forces of a personal vision and the
things or people that tend to influence our life.
By standing firm we will gain life. (Luke 21:19)

Resist the pressures of opposition by encouraging
yourself in the Lord our God. Sometimes others'
remarks must be ignored. Take courage to
continue in the face of pressure.

Michael Marnu

Subdue the inner person

I know that a feeling of rejection develops when people we trust lack confidence, belittle, misunderstand or criticise us. The threats of our circumstances and troubles may strike fear in us that may intimidate us. Our loved ones may rebel or hold pain or bitterness against us, waiting for the opportunity to avenge. If we allow rejection to affect us, our faith will be paralysed. It can cut deep into our soul, causing wounds that may remain for many years.

Everything we do starts inside. Before we can effectively influence the difficulties that confront us, we must first subdue the negatives that undoubtedly still reside within us. There are three powerful kingdoms within us which we must conquer to become leaders of influence: rejection; the threat of fear and the bitterness of betrayal by friends or family members.

No matter people's low perception about us, let us find sufficiency in our precious God who sees us as jewels. We must confess God's words to subdue every critical and belittling word that is spoken against us. Regarding threats of our enemies, let our confidence in God's promises and faithfulness remain unshakable. When we seek God first, everything else comes into a new perspective; we see the situation from another point of view. Dennis Burke counsels that: 'Our past failures and mistakes do not have to dominate our present or future. Let us boldly take all those negative memories of the past and roll them to God. Please, do right and fear no man.

All out!

Finally, the way you look at life will determine how you perform. 'Anyone who puts a hand to the plough and then looks back is not fit for the kingdom of God'.(Luke 9:62) Abraham Lincoln, one of history's greatest men, was subject to failures. Aged 22, his business failed. At 23 he ran for Legislature and was defeated. At 24 he tried to set up another business but it failed. At 25 he was elected to the Legislature. At 26, his sweetheart died. At 27 he had a nervous breakdown. At 34 he ran for Congress and was defeated. At 37 he re-ran for Congress and was elected. At 39 he ran again for Congress and was defeated. At 46 he ran for Senate and was defeated. At 47 he ran for vice-president and was defeated. At 49 he ran again for Senate and was defeated. At 51, he ran for president and was elected to become the greatest president of the USA.

The road to success is uphill all the way. It will take you time to get there often by way of multiple defeats. People will murmur, complain and challenge your authority. You may face bitter and violent opposition; endure physical affliction, mental turmoil or experience criti-cism and loneliness. Opposition is bound to arise but perseverance is the key. It is a brave man person that confronts the difficulties and contends against them. It is your tenacity that will hold you up under the pressure of waiting for the difficulty to disperse or a breakthrough to arise. The brave man does not swerve from his direction even in the greatest crises or suffering. Tenacity is a virtue that grows under crisis.

Perseverance is necessary in our walk with Christ. We may enter into the kingdom of God through many tribulations. (Acts 14:22) Jesus forewarns us not to look back. He 'who puts his hand to the plough and then looks back is not fit for the kingdom of God.' (Luke 9:62) Never say die. The righteous will move onward and forward'. (Job 17:9)

7

A DREAMER

Heather Wraight and Pat Wraight writing on the stories of churches that refused to die observed one important factor. Leaders can either make or break any situation. It was depressing to realise that ineffective or ill leaders had been the cause of decline in several churches. Vision and leadership, when they go hand in hand and are bathed in prayer are probably the most important factors in turning around a church, whether it is on the brink of extinction, on a steady downward decline or has been stagnating for several years. Such leaders are able to think and act strategically and to promote strategic action.

The anatomy

I learnt long ago that every successful vision has a structure and for dreams to become reality all its varied functions must be active. Pat Mesiti has likened the structure of a successful dreamer to the human body. The human body is not made up of one part but of many. These parts of the human body are varied in function. Just as the human body needs all its components to function as it is intended to, a dreamer needs all of the characteristics to move ahead.

- The mind – foundation, substance, moral values and character lie behind a dreamer. He is in forward – or positive gear. He is a creative thinker, diligent, persevering, coming up with solutions and not dwelling on problems.
- The eyes and ears – he sees the future, the present as it can be, opportunities and hope in hopelessness and destiny in despair. He is focussed.
- The tongue – he speaks words of encouragement. He is optimistic and speaks positively. He chooses words wisely. He is able to communicate, affirm, respect and impart the dream.
- The backbone – He plans for the dream. He turns dreams into goals – years, months, weeks and days. He goes for goals that are specific,

measurable, action-oriented, realistic and timetabled.

- The hands – he is the 'doing hands' that get done what needs to be done. He is a hard worker, not lazy, doesn't point the finger and is free from excuses.
- The heart – He is love and compassion for others, not ruthless. He doesn't carry hurt, contributes to others and maintains high standards. He's honest, never quits, learns from hard times and works together with others.
- The stomach – he stays away from junk-negative magazines, newspapers, movies and critical friends. He allows free-flowing thoughts and doesn't stifle tradition but laments small mindedness.
- The legs and feet – their feet run through challenges rather than from them, sidestepping obstacles, out-manoeuvring hindrances and leaping over temporary setbacks.

The eyes of success
'The eyes are the window of the soul; Keep your mouth shut and your eyes open'. Some succeed, others fail. Perhaps one reason is that successful people's eyes see where failure cannot. To write history, you must see the future, the present as it can be: opportunities, hope in hopelessness and destiny in despair.

We must see differently and beyond the facts. We need to see the future for our community, business, family, and so on, so that we are able to deal with the challenges we face now.

Dreamers are focused and thereby are able to aim, like an arrow, at a single target, writes Pat Mesiti. They know who they are and where they want to go and keep focused on that goal until they get there. It is said that when Henry Ford wanted to produce a V8 engine his engineers said it was impossible. 'Produce it anyway. Keep working. I want it and I'll have it', instructed Henry. At long last, it worked out. It took 18 years for Henry to build the motorcar.

You have a desire to be successful in life. There's no reason why not. It boils down to many things. For now, 'Do you look beyond circumstances and avoid being distracted.' Just as Jesus endured the cross and its scorning shame – the humiliation of its suffering – because, just as runners concentrate on the finishing line, He focused on prospects of future glory, so we also should concentrate on the goal and objective of our purpose in life.

The arms, hands and legs of a dreamer
Charles Darwin, the son of a country doctor, did not do particularly well at school. He was unable to settle to prepare himself for any profession. His father was reputed to have said, 'you are good for nothing but shooting guns and rat-catching ... you'll be a disgrace

to yourself and all of your family.' At the age of 22, Charles became the ship's naturalist on HMS Beagle, which left England for a five-year voyage in 1831. During the voyage, Darwin collected hundreds of specimens and made many observations about the variety of organisms and the ways in which they had adapted to their environments. He gained much information, in particular, from the variety of life forms in South America and the Galapagos Islands. In 1859, he published his now famous book The Origin of the Species. This book changed forever the way in which biologists think about how species arise. Charles Darwin worked hard to write history. He collected and observed hundreds of specimens.

Dreamers succeed when they have 'doing hands' that do what needs to be done. There is no excuse for avoiding hard work. All worthwhile dreams require as much perspiration as they do inspiration, writes Pat Mesiti. Furthermore, a dreamer's feet run through challenges rather than from them, sidestepping obstacles, out-manoeuvring hindrances and leaping over temporary setbacks. He gets back on his feet after being knocked down.

Jesus was a hard worker. (Acts 10:38) He sought His clients everywhere. Hard work is an antidote to poverty. If laziness turns us from our responsibilities, poverty may soon after bar us from the legitimate rest we should enjoy. We benefit if we are industrious and do the best work we can do (Ecclesiastes 9:10; 1 Kings 11:28). Honest, hard work is much better than schemes to get rich quickly. (Proverbs 13:11)

The tongue of a dreamer

Think about this, 'dreams live or die in our mouths'. As God created the world with words, we can either create or kill with words, with little effort. All that it takes are kind or harsh words. A dreamer kills his dream in his own mouth if he does not realise that the ability to control his tongue is a clear mark of wisdom; that his tongue has the power of life and death.

The words we use and the thoughts and attitudes behind them determine our future. We should be able to communicate the dream, affirm the dream, respect the dream and impart the dream. By so doing we are able to help others assimilate the dream. Our words matter to God (Psalm 15: 1-3); only those who speak rightly can enter His presence. Our words show what kind of a person we really are. 'If we claim to be religious but don't control our tongue, we are just fooling ourselves, and our religion is worthless.' (James 1:26) Since the tongue is so difficult to control, anyone who controls it perfectly gains control of himself in all other areas of life as well. It is always hard to argue with someone who insists on answering gently. Contrarily, a raised voice and harsh words almost always trigger an angry response.

Birds are entangled by their feet, and men by their tongue. A good tongue is a good weapon. We must commit ourselves wholeheartedly to talk about God's promises and our dreams on a continual basis. We must try to help others and build them up by what we say (Job 16:5; Ephesians 4:29) giving good advice when the right time comes (Proverbs 25:11) and speaking words of thanks and praise to one another and to God. (Psalm 50:23)

Hand-picked for a special purpose

Think about this, 'Guglielmo Marconi (1874–1937) is the father of radio communication. He transferred wireless waves, from a scientific curiosity, to an entirely new form of communication. In 1896, aged 22, he took out the world's first patent for wireless telegraphy. In 1901 he astonished the world by sending wireless signals over the Atlantic from Poldhu in Cornwall, England, to St. John's Newfoundland, Canada. He received honours and decorations from many countries and was awarded the Nobel Prize for Physics in 1909. When he died in 1937, the Italian government gave him a state funeral and radio stations all over the world fell silent for two minutes in his honour.

The stage was set for great minds like Marconi, Baird (television), Edison (electric light) and Bell (telephone); they chose their arrows with conviction and shot with precision, no wonder time will always freeze to remember what they did in history. Think about this, 'When the Lord

God made the earth and heaven ... for the Lord God had not sent rain on the earth and there was no man to work the ground ...'. (Genesis 2: 4-7) There are no spare parts in humans. We have been hand-picked and placed on this earth for a special purpose. We all have a definite part to play, although it may as yet not be clear what part or role each of us is to play. Your role will be suited to your gifts, talents, abilities, weaknesses and personality. We must take the once-in-a lifetime initiative, one that invites everyone to make and keep a simple heartfelt goal or commitment and record it for life. Everything counts. Singly or together we must make a positive difference.

Unlock your full potential

Zoe Koplowitz has suffered from multiple sclerosis for the past 25 years. Despite her illness, she has run 11 marathons, several in New York, one in Boston and the last in London. A British newspaper echoed her performances by saying, 'Brave Zoe defies risk of coma to finish the 26- mile course on crutches'. Zoe has become a heroine by turning her situation around to raise awareness for multiple sclerosis. She says, 'I am a reminder that anything in life is possible. Whatever you think you can't do, think of me and know that you can.'

Are you feeling tied down by cares and responsibilities, circumstances and afflictions? If so, learn something from Zoe and people like her. The English poet, John Milton, wrote better poetry when he became blind. The composer, Ludwig Beethoven, composed better music when he was deaf. The naturalist, Charles Darwin changed the scientific concept of life on earth, even though he was an invalid. It is important to have a sense of direction, for without a personal goal, life may seem aimless and purposeless. Secondly, realise that it is our thoughts about life, not our circumstances themselves that determine our future. Many people live with frustration and are held captive because they have put a negative lid on their potential. Thirdly, having the right attitude ensures that you reach your maximum effectiveness and good results inevitably follow. People who succeed do not wait until conditions are perfect before they make their mark. Life responds to the way you think. How you think determines how you act. Therefore renew your mind. (Romans 12:2)

God sees you as serene, confident and cheerful. We are all made to win. Wake up and live.

8

THE FAILURE FACTOR

The animated films of Walt Disney have delighted people of all ages since the first talking films appeared in cinemas in 1928. In 1955 Disney opened Disneyland, a large amusement park at Anaheim, California. It is said that Disney approached 300 banks and financial institutions before he got the backing to build Disneyland. He died in Los Angeles in 1966 having won 30 Academy Awards.

The Nigerians have a saying, 'A hunter who has only one arrow does not shoot with careless aim.' Unlike the cat, which is thought by some to have nine lives, we humans have only one life, the significance of which should be self-evident. It is somewhat disheartening that many people waste their lives, impeded by frustration, emptiness, disgust, hopelessness, apathy and anger. They don't believe in themselves and always expect the worst for themselves. They are always worried about how they look, what others will think of them or whether they are going to fail in life.

Major causes of failure

Peter said that he would never disown Jesus despite Jesus' prediction. But when frightened, he went against all he had boldly promised. The story of Peter and many people who try earnestly and fail, compared to the few who succeed, is a great tragedy of life, writes Napoleon Hill who believes that many people fail in life because of one or a combination of factors.

The reasons for failure are manifold but according to Napoleon Hill there are discernable traits. An unfavourable hereditary background is one factor; people born with a deficiency of brainpower. A lack of a well-defined purpose in life promotes failure, those with no central purpose or definite goal at which to aim. A lack of ambition to aim above mediocrity, along with no desire to want to get ahead in life, or an unwillingness to pay the price of success, are other major reasons for failure. There is also the problem of insufficient education or ignorance – not knowing how to get what you want in life without violating the rights of others. It helps to know what to do with what we have. Lack of self-discipline is fatal to success. Failure is sent packing by our ability to control ourselves, which helps us to conquer all negative qualities because self-mastery is the hardest job. Besides, ill-health, unfavourable environmental influences during childhood bends the twig. Procrastination is another attribute of failure, for procrastination is the thief of time. Waiting for the 'right time' to start doing something worthwhile will never get the job done. Lack of persistence leads to poor finishing and a tendency to give up at the first signs of defeat. A negative personality repels the cooperative efforts of other people so that their valuable contribution to your life may be lost. Uncontrolled sexual urges and the desire for 'something for nothing', an unwillingness to sow in tears or pay the price for success, are other factors to ensure failure. (Psalm 126:3) Lack of decision-making ability, the wrong association and over-caution are other things to avoid if you want to welcome success.

Be aware of your own breaking point and do not become over-confident or self-sufficient. Remember that Peter's humiliating experience taught him much about how to become an effective leader of the Christian movement. (Luke 22:62) Intentional dishonesty is fatal when pursuing a political career. There is no hope for people who are dishonest because dishonest deeds soon catch up with them. Egotism and vanity lead to selfishness, pride and over-confidence, all of which repel people. Successful people keep an open mind and are afraid of nothing, while intolerance and closed mindedness give wings to opportunities. Intemperance, especially over-indulgence in eating, drinking and sex, are also fatal to success. We may fail if we are in an occupation we cannot throw ourselves into wholeheartedly, because enthusiasm is convincing, contagious and attracts people to our fold; lack of enthusiasm is always a bad sign. There is always the temptation to become a 'jack of all trades', which means you become the master of nothing. Those who enjoy spending sprees are seldom good at all, while poverty is a necessity that compels a person to sign a bad agreement. Possession of power when not acquired through self-effort is more dangerous than foolishness. An ability to cooperate with others is essential, while acting on 'opinions' created by guesswork or snap judgments weakens the path to success. Do not be too lazy to acquire facts that help you to think accurately and back-up your knowledge.

After Israel had been cleansed from Achan's sin, Joshua prepared to attack Ai again, this time to win. (Joshua 8:1) Joshua had learnt his lesson. The lessons we learn from our failures should make us better and able to handle the same situation the second time around. The oldest admonition is 'know yourself', writes Napoleon Hill, to build bridges. You can tell what kind of a person you are by what you do on the second and third attempts.

Failure is caused by having no reason why you want to achieve your goal. Having no reason or purpose for what you are doing is also a cause for failure. Impatience is fatal to success, doing things fast and easy, shying away from the difficult and time-consuming tasks. Unrealistic expectations in outcome and time can be very discouraging. Many people fear change but all growth involves some form of change. For things to change you must appropriately initiate change in yourself and how you do things. Failing to write your vision down is fatal. God told Habakkuk, 'write down the revelation and make it plain on tablets so that a herald may run with it.' (Habakkuk 2:2-3) Writing crystallises thought and thought motivates action. By putting your goals down on paper you are creating a psychological commitment, which allows you to set your priorities, deadlines and look for balance. Lack of commitment is a hindrance to achievement; until there is commitment there will always be a way back or a way to avoid doing what is essential to your goal and success. No plan. No reward system. No imagination. Nothing can be accomplished without being mentally accomplished first. See yourself in it. Visualise the achievement. No action: so we must do whatever it takes for without action, all good intentions are tales. Take a new step by giving up familiar but limiting patterns, safe but unrewarding work, values you no longer believe in and relationships that have lost their meaning, writes Bob Gass, for

'If you think you can just hold your ground and still make progress, you are mistaken'.

He that stays in the valley, shall never get over the hill. Five of the biggest lessons I learnt from my role as a general overseer of Wembley International Christian Centre, in which I would like to amplify, before concluding this chapter, are as follows:

- Begging off
- Procrastination
- Excuses
- Passing the bucks
- Self-pity

We are all prone to taking the course of least resistance, of escaping responsibility. Marriage, parenting, leadership, work, along with many other human activities, are fraught with the challenge of duty or responsibility. There may be more troubles than gains when taking up one's duty, yet begging off is no excuse. Stop seeking release. There are always serious consequences to begging off such as unhappiness, loneliness or guilt. (Hebrews 12:25, 28)

Whatever you can do or dream you can, begin it. The habit of putting things off has become one of the factors preventing people from achieving. Procrastination is the thief of time. The passing of time never makes action easier, quite the opposite. Delay is the deadliest form of denial and when you say later to something that is important to you, you are cheating yourself out of your success for inheritance.

Sleeping and tiredness are very popular delaying tactics, which usually manifest themselves when you are close to doing something difficult or uncomfortable. Nevertheless, a lazy man is never lucky. Do not rationalise by saying you have to do it properly. Just completing something by doing it is 100 per cent better than doing well at something you never even start. A bad idea acted on is 100 per cent better than a good idea not acted on. 'As long as it is day, we must do the work of Him who sent us. Night is coming, when no one can work.' (John 9:4)

Stop making excuses and realise your dreams today. There is a parable about a man who was hosting a great supper and sent his servant to say to those he had invited, 'Come, for all is now ready'. All the intended guests began making excuses and begging off. Three amazing excuses were made for not attending the party, not one of which was impressive. One excused himself saying he was testing oxen that night, but we all know that no one tests oxen at night. Another excused himself saying that he had just got married, although a dinner would have been a nice outing for a newly wed couple. The third guest excused himself saying he needed to inspect a piece of land that night, but why would you do such a job at night? Many people are full of excuses. Many excuses cannot be substantiated. They are empty and full of lies.

Excuses appear in a wide variety of forms but the worst type, according to David J. Schwartz, are those that involve health, intelligence, age and luck – 'My health is not good'; 'You've got to have brains to succeed'; 'It's no use, I am too old'; 'I am too young to try that' or 'But my case is different; I attract bad luck'. What differentiates the successful from the unsuccessful is their ability to avoid making excuses. Study the lives of successful people to discover that high-achievers do not make excuses as mediocre people tend to.

I always remember this when I am tempted to make an excuse to get out of something: 'excuses are mind-deadening; a disease of your thoughts'. Fear is often at the root of an excuse, so each time I pull back from an opportunity with an excuse, there is another brick in the wall that keeps me from reaching my life goal. Opportunity is only a visitor; I don't assume it will revisit tomorrow. I move while the door is open. 'The lazy person is full of excuses.' (Proverbs 22:13)

I have drawn the boundary where 'the buck stops'. It has been observed that, each year, about 20 million civil lawsuits are filed in United States. The majority of lawsuits are filed by people looking to blame someone else for irresponsible, careless actions. How easy it is to fall into the trap of blaming others.

There are two kinds of people on the road of life: Passengers and drivers. People who take responsibility are the drivers of the world; people who do not take responsibility are the passengers. The drivers are in control of their lives. The passengers are just along for a ride, watching the world to go by instead of participating. Passengers are backseat drivers, guessing and telling the drivers where they should have turned, instead of getting behind the wheel themselves. Are you the driver or the passenger in your own life? Being the driver in your life, according to Burke Hedges, is what separates the adults from the children.

Many people live with frustration because of their reliance on others. We can acknowledge the fact that we are not responsible for what happens to us, but we are responsible for the way we respond to what happens to us. It is not so much what happens to us but what we do as a consequence that matters. We can never blame God, pastors, politicians, the world economy, parents, friends or anybody else for our lives. The only person to blame for your own state of affairs is yourself. You can never make yourself better by blaming everything on somebody else.

Remember the words of Helen Keller and Mary McCarthy. 'I am only one, but still I am one; I cannot do everything, but still I can do something; I will not refuse to do the something I can do.' Life isn't about finding yourself, life is about creating yourself. Let the buck stop here.

It is amazing how much my life has been shaped by the decision to handle failure proactively. Aldous Huxley once wrote, 'Experience is not what happens to you; it is what you do with what happens to you'. I have met with failure and survived. Even when failure is immense, I refuse to lie in the dust and bemoan my tragedy. I have come to understand the law of the second chance and sometimes the third and fourth. The worth of a man is measured by his life, not by his failure under a singular and peculiar trial. No failure need be final, whether it is our own failure or someone else's. I have always believed that a good challenge presents new opportunities – opportunities to learn, to grow, to gain strength, or to reach a higher goal. Failure and opportunity are two sides of the same coin. Opportunity is next door to failure.

No one is perfect, and we cannot be right all the time. The biggest sin of all is not failure but quitting. When you quit there is nothing God can do. Our future which is in God's hands is good and pleasing. (Jeremiah 29:11) Use your difficult time to put your life in order and on a proper footing. When you are knocked down, bounce back, learn a lesson, forget the beating and move upward. Never think defeat. We may encounter setbacks but should not surrender to them. We can overcome big and real obstacles. Refuse to become a martyr to your circumstances. Avoid self-pity; self-pity is a 'social cancer' that can trap you into a miserable cycle of complaining whining and whimpering. It is not possible to win a high level of success without reacting positively to your circumstances.

To handle failure does require wisdom. 'If the axe is dull and its edge unsharpened, more strength is needed' but skill will bring success. (Ecclesiastes 10:10) Remember that God holds all wisdom in His hands. (Job 28: 12, 21)

9

Highway to success

Charles Darwin, the son of a country doctor, did not do particularly well at school. He was unable to settle to prepare himself for any profession. His father was reputed to have said: 'you are good for nothing but shooting guns and rat-catching ... you will be a disgrace to yourself and all of your family.' In 1859, he published his now famous book The Origin of the Species, and changed the scientific concept of the earth's creation. Likewise, in adversity, Milton wrote better poetry when he became blind and Beethoven composed better music when he was deaf.

Taking an overview of various biographies and autobiographies it becomes clear that many of the world's most brilliant achievers faced difficult circumstances. Charles Darwin, Winston Churchill, Helen Keller, Hollard Sanders, Ray Crock, Stephen Spielberg, Walt Disney, Richard Branson, Bill Gates and many others, are proof that 'even when life is against you, you can still get out there and make a go of it'. Irrespective of how average you think you are, how ordinary you may feel, or how ineffective you consider your life, you can change your world. It is the 'average' people who write history. We can change our world if we make up our mind to do that and make a decision not to become a victim of our circumstances. Grasp the fact that we are created for greatness, that we are incredibly creative, emotional beings. Realise that it is not what happens or has happened to us in life that counts but how we respond to what happens that is important. Wake up from the slumber of the status quo that has conditioned you.

God has a purpose for each person, some are appointed for specific works. Faith calls on us to respond, to take God at His word and advance into an unknown future relying on His enabling protection. Go for it, He is counting on us.

The American, scientist, inventor, businessman and inventor of the light bulb – Thomas Edison – was sent away from school because the teacher thought his continual questions were a sign of stupidity. His first great interest was chemistry and he read all he could about it; he was only ten when he began to grow and sell vegetables so that he could buy chemicals for making experiments in the cellar. When he was 12 he worked selling magazines and fruits on a train and began printing a weekly newspaper on a printing press set up in a luggage van. In 1869 he went to New York; he had no friends there and was in debt, but he had the luck to walk into the Telegraph Company building just as the telegraph stopped working. He was the only person who could put it right and, as a result, he was employed by the company. The rest is history.

The unquestionable ability of a person to elevate his life by conscious endeavour is reassuring. Once you have decided to wake up, you need to create your dream. Be prepared to capitalise on the next opportunity that presents itself or, better still, create a list of opportunities. Every dream begins with a concept. Its formation, incubation and birth follow. Do not wait for the big break: conceive your dream now; nurture your project through gestation; give form to it, help it grow and watch its birth. Although the risk of being misunderstood is common for those embarking on new projects, allow your dream to grow in stages and stick with it.

Interestingly, those with ordinary talents often achieve more than those with greater physical and intellectual endowments, simply because they have learnt to work harder with what they have. Thomas Edison himself said that he owed his success to hard work rather than any great intellectual ability.

How to be a winner!
'To Be' or 'To Do'

Nicodemus, a member of the Jewish ruling council, came to Jesus at night to find out what he could do to have eternal life. (John 3:1-15) In reply Jesus declared, 'I tell you the truth, no-one can see the kingdom of God unless he is born again'. Nicodemus was impressed with Jesus' miracles, but faith based on miracles alone is not enough. There must be inner cleansing, a complete change of heart brought about by the creative power of the Spirit of God. Only then can a person enter the kingdom. (John 3:1-5; Ezekiel 36:25-27)

Think about this, 'Fishes swim as birds fly. Lions eat meat because they are carnivores.' Jesus was not concerned with physical birth as He chatted to Nicodemus. Jesus was talking about the work of God's spirit that gives repentant sinners new life and enables them to enter God's kingdom. Like the wind, the work of the Spirit is mysterious. It cannot be seen, though its results certainly can. (John 3: 6-8) In the words of Dag Heward Mills, 'when you see a successful minister, look beyond the physical and see into the realm of the spirit. Observe the anointing at work. There is an invisible cloak over the person which allows him to succeed in what he is doing. That invisible mantle is what I call the anointing. It explains why some people succeed and some don't. It explains why some people have a greater degree of success under exactly the same circumstances...' The Holy Bible hits the nail on the head when it states the secret of Jesus' success: 'how God anointed Jesus of Nazareth with the Holy Spirit and power, and how he went around doing good and healing all who were under the power of the devil, because God was with him.' (Acts 10:38) Isaiah also confirmed the power of 'To be' as a secret of success when he wrote, 'In that day their burden will be lifted from your shoulders, the yoke from your neck; the yoke will be broken because you have grown so fat' (the anointing). (Isaiah 10:27)

Many people believe that success is more 'To be' than 'To do'. The 'To do' school believes that success does not come by accident. The individual that seeks success must first realise that what you get will depend on how much you put into it. 'Press towards the goal' is their maxim. The 'To be' school of thought believes that the secret to success is more of an inherent quality a person possesses. It is therefore imperative to develop these qualities or habits. An instance is that of Jesus Christ. Luke 2:40 and 52 unveils Jesus' success like this: 'And the child grew and became strong; he was filled with wisdom, and the grace of God was upon him'. (Luke 2:40) 'And Jesus grew in wisdom and stature, and in favour with God and men.' (Luke 2:52) Nevertheless 'To be' and 'To do' like two sides of a coin are different facets of success.

'To Be'

'To be' as a facet of success is a term I have coined to describe the innate ability a person has. (Proverb 18:16) It is the foundation, a support, that 'something' that does not wither away but remains constant and gives the person stability in the midst of the cyclone of disaster. When life turns upside down, when calamity strikes – things over which we often have no control, it is how we deal with the calamity that makes the difference. 'To be' is a value on the inside of a person that shapes what they do on the outside. It is who they are on the inside. It is the internal quality of a person, the strength of a person, which is not demonstrated in how much they can do but in how much they can bear in the midst of adversity. It is not something you can boast about, it is forged through the adversities of life. (Proverbs 24:10) Failure is something that none of us likes. But it comes to us all the same. A person of solid foundation would not give up because they have the fuel to help them rise from the flames of failure. (Proverbs 24:16) They may fall seven times and rise up again and again and again.

'To be' is developed or perceived in the character of a person but shines outwards, eclipsing what they do to achieve success. It is a priceless gift. However, like every invaluable thing, it is developed from years of consistent and diligent behaviour. It demands effort, time, perseverance and commitment. It will come only to those who make it a priority in their lives. Such a desire overcomes the inertia which results from our natural laziness and excuses. It is imperative that we take a step back to assess our values, opinions and beliefs to discern whether they are true, just, and pure as they are capable of bringing life-changing and life-enhancing results, writes Andrew Rashford-Hewitt.

Winning requires people of wisdom, strength, favour with God and people of right attitude.

Wisdom

To turn your minuses into pluses requires wisdom and intelligence. We need wisdom to see difficulties in a true light and to profit from them. Difficulties often overwhelm us and create struggles that require wisdom to resolve them. We need a wisdom that enables us to meet life and its difficulties with decision and action. It is that queenly regulative discretion that sees and selects worthy ends and the best means of attaining them.

Wisdom cries out to us every day (Proverbs 8:1) and it is of great urgency, a wise king once wrote. He who exalts her will be promoted. (Proverbs 4:8) She protects. (Proverbs 2:16) A wise man will recognise the potential temptation, foresee the inevitable consequences, consequences that often never go away. Living by wise pointers will mean that we avoid pitfalls, helping us not to limp and stumble along. (Proverbs 4:12) The fruit will be development and steady progress as we run the race of life. Wisdom makes wise planning which will watch over us and keep us safe. (Proverbs 2:11) It has been observed that planning helps cope with life events, our directions and our ambitions. Wise planning considers many options and with insight makes a superior decision to those made on the spur of the moment, writes Andrew Rashford-Hewitt. Wisdom creates. As rightly observed by King Solomon (Proverbs 3:19), the creation of this world was not based upon the evolution theory but rooted in the sovereign wisdom of God. In truth, wisdom will multiply our days and add years to our life. (Proverbs 9:11) Think about this, 'For whoever finds me finds life and wins approval from the Lord. But those who miss me have injured themselves. All who hate me love death'. (Proverbs 8:35-36)

Life is about choices. The ability to make wise choices will usually result in progress, reduction in stress, increased sense of peace and development, all of which are life enhancing. 'When wisdom entered thy heart and knowledge is pleasant unto thy soul discretion shall preserve thee and understanding shall keep thee. To deliver you from the way of the evil men who leave the path of uprightness to walk in the ways of darkness', writes King Solomon. (Proverbs 2: 10-13) In truth one way to become a failure is to plod in life without wisdom and in ignorance.

Personal intuition

Sometimes situations and circumstances may seem so difficult that we wonder what to do and have to seek more information or advice. Most of the answers to what we need and want to know lie within each of us, however, and can be obtained by listening to our personal intuition. Think about this, 'The seed of a plant has the propensity to produce a new plant and contains within it an embryo that consists of an immature root and stem. From the embryo the mature plant develops. 'Just as seeds grow into flowers and fruits, we all have within us an inner pattern or blueprint for perfection. By its nature this pattern is unique, special to each individual. We will naturally feel more joyful and fulfilled when we follow what is the perfect outworking of our inner pattern.' (Patricia Cleghorn)

Personal intuition is vital for success, and guides us to do what is best. Personal intuition is the inner voice that, like a road sign, directs you as you travel down the road with no clear idea of where you are going and with no light to guide you. Without the inner voice you are bound to be lost. As you listen to your personal intuition you know what is right for you; your inner voice tells you, 'this is right for me'. Carrying out an action guided by your inner voice can seem like an unusual step, but personal intuition protects you from doing things that are not respectful towards yourself and others. It can stop you from saying 'yes' when you want to say 'no'. Using your personal intuition puts you in touch with your purpose in life and helps you evaluate what is important.

Some of the ways God speaks to us are through our inner convictions or 'hunches'; by the desires of our heart (Psalm 37:4) and through the inner, still, and small voice of the Holy Spirit. (Acts 11:12; Acts 13:2) We even have the anointing of God abiding within us. (1 John 2:27; Ephesians 3:17) The anointing is the place of power where sickness and disease, depression, and other ailments are destroyed. (Isaiah 10:27) Once personal intuition becomes a reality no problem is able to prevail over us.

Strength
Stature or strength is more than the physical power one has in ones body. It is the intensity or the ability to withstand pressure – physical, emotional even spiritual. The reality of winning life is demonstrated by its reaction under adversity. Read the biographies and autobiographies of successful people and you discover that each of these people has encountered opposition, discouragement, setbacks and personal misfortune. As you drive towards your destiny, you will hit potholes and take wrong turns. The only way to avoid them is to never leave your drive way. Nevertheless, one of the essential ingredients of an effective

person is his problem-solving capacity. Almost everything we do involves problem-solving in one way or another. This might be regarded as one of the differences between being a loser and being a winner. It is rather unfortunate that problem-solving is the most difficult task for many people. No doubt many people are frustrated and stressed.

Assume personal responsibility for the way you are. We can acknowledge the fact that we are not responsible for what happens to us, but we are responsible for the way we respond to what happens to us. It is not so much what happens to us as what we do with it that matters. With right attitude every setback can become a springboard, and every stumbling block a stepping stone.

Are you in times of great distress, suffering, hardship or difficulty? Then remember these: In our daily lives there shall be times that we shall face problems. These problems come at an undetermined time. View these problems as challenges. If you react properly to the situation, the situation itself shall give you more strength, power and ability you do not ordinarily possess. If you react improperly to the situation, the situation can rob you of the skill, control and ability that you ordinarily have to call upon. Identify the cause of your problem to determine the solution. Do not waste time ruminating on the problem, worrying about what will happen next and questioning why it happened in the first place. Treat your problem as urgent. Find a solution to it. Remember always that 'None of the circumstances and adversities we face is responsible for creating stress. It is how we react to our circumstances and adversity that activates stress in our lives.

Favour

There is another key to success: the favour of God. Favour means to give special regard to; to treat with goodwill; to show exceptional kindness to someone. It means to show extra kindness in comparison to the treatment of others; that is, preferential treatment. It sometimes simply means that the one favoured is shown kindness and treated with a generosity and goodwill far beyond what would normally be expected. He is treated much better than he could expect. It is from this use of favour that we get the word, favourite. The greatest favours are shown to the favourite.

A psalmist said that the favour of God was the difference between life and death. (Psalm 30:5-7) So it is important, even vital, that we find the favour of God. People will favour us because God's favour has hooked them in. They're stuck. It makes it seem almost like there has been a long, deep friendship with the person giving favour when, in fact, you may have only known him or her a short time. People do you good not out of pity or a benevolence they need from you or a good understanding of your plight. They seem to foresee your potential and the benefit thereof.

Mike Floyd in his book, Supernatural Success: Principles for Business Success, testifies how his business, which was in its lowest ebb and at the brink of bankruptcy, was turned around with impressive results. Drawing on the experiences of Abraham, Moses, Joseph, Daniel, Samuel, Jesus Christ and other men and women of God he was convinced that when our ways please God, we will have His favour and the favour of God opens doors no person can. God always makes a way where there seems to be no way.

God uses His power to protect those who trust in Him. He gives strength to those who are fully committed to Him. He even exercises His power through their weaknesses. He is the Most High God, the ruler and possessor of heaven and earth, the one who is in charge. He is the Almighty, all-powerful one; constantly pouring out nourishment to His children and meeting their needs. God's presence in our lives comes when we obey Him. (Acts 5:32; Leviticus 9:6; Titus 1:16) God wants us to do everything He commands us to do so that we will be prosperous and successful. (Joshua 1:9) If we are willing and obedient, we will eat the best from the land. (Isaiah 1:19) In all things, God works for the good of those who love Him. (Romans 8:28)

Hanna had been unable to conceive children and her barrenness caused her social embarrassment, for childlessness was considered a failure. Rather than dwelling upon her problem, Hanna prayed. She brought her problem honestly before God. The prayer opened the way for God to work in her favour.

God honours the desires of people who are faithful to Him with blessings. Blessings are God's divine power resting upon us which conveys favour, protection, delight, mercy, compassion, approval and peace on us. Blessings are an invincible vehicle of supernatural and spiritual power that produce good and beneficial results. Blessings are rarely limited to the individual and may be extended to generations or whole nations. There are many vehicles of blessings but the major one is words 'And God blessed them and said, be fruitful ...' (Genesis 1:28) which may be spoken, written or merely uttered.

Derek Prince has summed up blessings in the following groups: exaltation, health, reproduction, prosperity, victory and God's favour. God has promised great blessings to us. He will deliver us from fear; save us out of our troubles; guard and deliver us; show us goodness; supply our needs; listen when we talk to Him and redeem us. He blesses us in ways we do not expect. His blessings might not be immediate but they will come if we are faithful to what He says in His Word.

Right attitude – the winning spirit

There is, however, an indispensable key to success, attitude. Our perception of life is influenced by our attitude. If we filter our thoughts through a negative screen we end up being pessimistic; seeing the world as a gloomy and risky environment. With right attitude, the world is a 'bright, adventure-filled place overflowing with surprises and opportunities'. Bad attitude is like a toxic chemical. It is harmful and unfriendly. We have to get rid of it before it harms us.

Lennox Lewis became the undisputed heavyweight champion of the world on 15 November 1999 after ten years of effort. He encountered setbacks but did not surrender to them. He knew that it was not possible to achieve high-level success without meeting opposition. This is a demonstration of the winning spirit, the only thing that separates tragedy from victory. In times of crisis, the winning spirit is crucial.

During a setback, the winning spirit focuses on the positives instead of the negatives; it positions itself to end up as a winner. The person with a winning mentality is the one who is aware of personal defects but knows the importance of maintaining the right attitude. He refuses to let his personal struggles rob him of his destiny. He has not only learnt to live with his weakness but also learned how to conquer it continually. The winning spirit is invincible: setbacks become springboards; obstacles become opportunities and barriers become blessings. The coward becomes a conqueror and writes history. A winning spirit is comparable to a kite: the harder the wind blows, the more it rises. The winning spirit lifts a person above his circumstances so that he is able to handle anything.

The winning spirit comes to those who remain focused on the task at hand and the promise of blessing to come. Being mentally alert (preparing the mind for action), disciplined (self-controlled), and focused (set our hope fully), we gather up our long, flowing garments and are poised ready for physical action. Our goals should absorb all our energy; nothing can make us take our eyes off our goals. With the single-mindedness of an athlete in training, we lay aside everything harmful and forsake anything that may distract us from being effective. (Philippians 3:13)

Two people in the same prison cell looked through the same prison bars but saw two different views. One saw mud whilst the other saw stars. One got broached and swamped with his circumstances, while the other rode his circumstances out, kept looking straight ahead and remained secure. One anchored his soul whilst the other anguished his soul. If the mental filter our thoughts pass through is negative we end up being pessimistic, viewing the world as a gloomy and risky environment.

With the positive mental filter, however, the world appears as a bright, adventure-filled place, overflowing with surprises and opportunities.

One of the characteristics of a successful person is a positive attitude: this gives them the ability to attain maximum effectiveness from which good results inevitably follow. A positive attitude is the winning spirit, a motivational characteristic which is comparable to the fearless bravery of 'the people of war'. The people of war are trained for battle and are not afraid to fight as they have developed strategies for winning. They have that 'bulldog spirit' which rises above all fear and circumstances. While others treat their swords as ornaments, the people of war are mentally equipped to march into the enemy's camp and take everything that has been stolen. The person with these sorts of qualities is purpose-driven; he does not just survive but he overcomes. He understands that while adversity or problems may strike they cannot bury him underneath their weight. All the water in the ocean won't sink him! He keeps his vision alive and he's willing to pay the price. He is willing to wait for it and work for it. He will always leave his safety zone and go where others are fearful to tread. Things that would break the loser only motivate the winning spirit to break through and even break records.

By keeping our eyes on Jesus – on whom our faith depends from start to finish – we can harbour the winning spirit. Just as a runner concentrates on the finishing line, we should concentrate on Christ, the goal and objective of our faith. Do not stumble or look away from Him to stare at yourself or your circumstances; run for Christ, not yourself, and always keep Him in sight.

'To do'

Remember how Evander Holyfield amazed the world when he beat Mike Tyson to win the World Heavyweight Boxing title! He was not a good bet but with courage and faith in God, he made the impossible possible to reach the highest heights in the boxing world. His motto was: 'I can do all things through Christ that strengthens me.' (Philippians 4:13)

Many principles have been observed as the keys to success: the intense desire for success; a clear sighted attitude; the setting up of moderately difficult (not impossible) goals; taking a realistic approach to risk (analysing and assessing problems); assuming personal responsibility to get the job done; being reckless and not worrying about failure. Successful people pay the price of their vision through hard work. Success thrives on opposition, so without discipline, vision remains dwarfed.

Everybody should have a vision

The heart of success is an intense desire for success and to be clear sighted. Clear sighted because successful people know where they are going and are confident of getting there.

Nothing much happens without a vision. And for something great to happen, there must be a great vision. For behind every great achievement is a dreamer. Where there is no vision, people get out of hand. When you've no personal goal which you are interested in, which means something to you, you are bound to go around in circles, feel lost and disillusioned, life itself may seem aimless and purposeless. We should not live without vision. Can you imagine a politician without an election manifesto, or a military personnel without a campaign strategy, writes John Stott. Any attempt to achieve a goal in life without this recipe is like starting fire with water. It won't work.

Vision, as a recap, is compounded of a deep dissatisfaction with what is and a clear grasp of what could be. It begins with indignation over the status quo, and it grows into the earnest quest for an alternative. Think about this: 'We see the unacceptable: do we not care? We see what is: do we not see what could be? Things could be different. We need a vision of purpose.' Feeling sorry for circumstance would get us nowhere. We must dream about all the things we'd like to accomplish.

There is a serious dearth of visionaries and dreamers. These are the people with a 'hunch' alternatives, those who believe that it is possible to build a better world. They are people who are lovers of the earth, who feel a responsibility for life and wish to give true meaning to their lives and to the lives of others. They are the pathfinders of life or live to represent a growing ground-swell of change, concludes John Stott.

Sow in tears and reap in joy

There is one success ingredient often found in men of valour but missing in many people. This is the ability to get things done or to get results. Every big job requires a vision and a man who thinks of action. Excellent ideas are not enough. Only a few ideas acted upon and developed is 100 pr cent better than a terrific idea that dies because it was not followed up. Many people have always been scornful of dreamers. The world is full of pessimistic people whose mind set is epitomised as following: 'Here comes that dreamer... come now let's kill him ... then we'll see what comes of his dreams ...' The dreams of the night tend to evaporate in the cold light of the morning.

Hard work is an indispensable trait of a winner

For this reason people who dare to dream need to become people of action. Action requires courage and hard work. Hard work is an indispensable trait of a winner. Think about this: 'In the words of Thomas Edison, 'genius is 1 per cent inspiration and 99 per cent perspiration' or the words of Thomas Carlyle 'the transcendent capacity of taking trouble'. The secret of genius is drudge. Hard work is an evident hallmark of history's successful people. Read the biographies and autobiographies of successful people and you discover that each of these people add hard work to vision. Thomas Edison made 1,000 experiments before he invented light. Kwame Nkrumah, the first Prime Minister and President of Ghana, political slogans went like this; ' Work and Happiness'.

Pay the price tag of the growth

A thriving life gives priority to growth and pays the price tag of the growth. If we think we can just hold our ground and still make progress, we're mistaken. The only way we can materialise our vision is hard work. Remember always that without the vision the campaign loses its direction and its fire, but without hard work and practical projects the dreams vanish into thin air. Dreams and reality, passion and practicalities must go together.

A lesser man gives up and abandons his vision to his own pettiness ...

In 1952, Kwame Nkrumah commenced the fight for Ghana's independence from British colonial rule. The road to independence was not set out on a silver platter. He rose to the highest position in the Gold Coast after spending over a year in prison. All because he had a dream. This is one of the characteristics of a winner. Perseverance does not swerve from the sense of direction by even the greatest crisis or suffering. It is the tenacity of life that holds up under pressure while waiting for dismissal of the difficulty or a breakthrough. Perseverance is an act of endurance or a frame of mind that bravely endures the difficulties and pressures encountered – the staying power. It is a virtue that grows under crisis.

Perseverance, however, does not present the picture of being under a heavy load and resolutely staying there instead of trying to escape. It is not a passive attitude of quiet submission or resignation but rather brave manliness that confronts the difficulties and contends against them. It is one thing to dream a dream and see visions. It is another to convert a dream into a plan of action. It is yet a third to persevere with it when opposition comes. Opposition is bound to arise. As the campaign gets under way, the forces of reaction muster, entrenched privilege digs itself in more deeply, commercial interest feels threatened and raises the alarm. In the words of John Stott, 'the cynical sneer at the folly of the "do-gooders" and apathy becomes transmitted into hostility'.

People will murmur, complain and challenge your authority. You may face bitter and violent opposition, endure physical affliction, suffer mentally or experience criticism and loneliness. A lesser person would give up and abandon them to their own pettiness. Those without the vision who are merely being carried along by the momentum of the campaign will soon capitulate. The pathfinder has the resilience to take setbacks in his stride, the tenacity to overcome fatigue and discouragement, and the wisdom to 'turn stumbling blocks into stepping stones'. Success thrives on opposition. Its silver is refined and its steel hardened, writes J.O. Sanders. Perseverance subjects itself to criticism. It listens to criticism, weighs it and modifies its programme accordingly. It does not, however, waver in the basic conviction of the vision. It always has its ideas intact and its standards uncompromising.

Are you contemplating giving up because of opposition, sacrifice or adversity. Then remember this: 'The road to success is uphill all the way. It will take you time to get there. Anything that is worth while is worth working for. The road to success is often through multiple defeats. Without pain and problem what real joy is there in progress. If it cost nothing, it means nothing.'

Without discipline, all the other gifts are dwarfs

Think about this: 'Even those who are young grow weak, young people can fall exhausted. Every vision has a tendency to fade. Every visionary is prone to discouragement. Hard work begun with zeal can easily degenerate into drudgery, suffering and loneliness take their toll. The leader feels and get tired. It takes discipline to master passion, time and energy and to finish the race'.

Before we can the get best out of life, discipline is inevitable. Without this quality, writes J. O. Sanders, all the other gifts remain as dwarfs; they cannot grow. Strong people, writes Peter

Drucker, always have strong weaknesses too. All successful people have fatal flaws. We are all made of flesh and blood. Even righteous Noah got drunk.

We are on the road to success when we learn to obey discipline imposed from without and take on a more rigorous discipline from within. Those who rebel against authority and scorn self-discipline do not qualify as winners. Many who are mediocre are sufficiently worthy in human standards, but have large areas of their life floating free from control. Lazy and disorganised people never get the best from life. J. O. Sanders writes, 'A person who desires to make the best out of life will work while others waste time, study while others snooze. Slothful habits are overcome, whether in thought or in deed. He eats right, stands tall and prepares himself to wage a good warfare. He will without reluctance undertake the unpleasant task that others avoid or the hidden duty that others evade, because it wins no public applause. He learns not to shrink from difficult situations or retreat from hard-edged people. He will not procrastinate, but will prefer to dispatch with the hardest tasks first. Without discipline, a little prudent compromise can sometimes be justified in our bid to fight the good fight to the end. Many things sound fine in theory but seem impractical. It is only those who discipline themselves keep their vision aglow'.

What stops us from fulfilling our vision

Can you imagine what stops us from fulfilling our vision? Scepticism, caution, fear, discouragement, doubt, excuses, procrastination and ignorance. In the words of Burke Hedges 'Well, by the time they turn the key of scepticism ... release the deadbolt of caution ... unlock the chains of fear ... and crack open the door, the once-in-lifetime opportunity is gone ...'

Do you want the best of life? Then remember that, ' Success in life is not the private possession of the brilliant scientist or the devoted theologian'. Success in life isn't something that happens to you. It is something that you yourself embark on, instead of relying on others or hoping to be lucky. If you want success to catch up with you or you think someone else might bring it to you, you are likely to have a long wait.

10

Personal empowerment and development

Once upon a time, a mentor wrote to his son, 'Study and be eager and do your utmost to present yourself ... approved, a workman has no cause to be ashamed, correctly analysing and accurately dividing the word of truth ...' then, consider the counsel of J. Oswald Sanders: 'Reading makes a full man; speaking a ready man; writing an exact man ... Lawyers must read steadily to keep up on case law. Doctors must read to stay current in the ever-changing world of healthcare. The opinion leaders must be well informed for effective guidance.'

People who reach their potential always think in terms of improvement. There is nothing worse than living a stagnant life devoid of improvement.

We need not be tomorrow what we are today. A thriving life always gives priority to growth and pays the price tag of personal growth. Our commitment to our goals determines how far we shall go. It has been my philosophy never to let the practice of studies to be on the wane because studies feed the soul and stimulate the mind. I study to refill the wells of inspiration, for intellectual and spiritual growth, to benefit and cultivate my confessions, to acquire new information, to keep current with the time and to be well informed.

I always take a new step by giving up familiar but limiting patterns, safe but unrewarding work, values I no longer believe in and relationships that have lost their meaning. If you think you can just hold your ground and still make progress, you are mistaken. The only way you can improve the quality of your life is to improve yourself. There are two areas of self-improvement which overlap and interweave. They are personal empowerment and personal development.

Personal empowerment
Literally the term 'empowerment' simply means becoming powerful. It is the means by which we are able to take control of our circumstances and achieve our purposes in life. By so doing we are able to work towards helping ourselves and others and maximise the quality of our lives. According to Thompson, through empowerment people can become better equipped to deal

with their problems and pursue their goals by having a firm grip over their circumstances, by becoming more aware of 'what makes us tick' and what our strengths and weaknesses are.

I have observed time and time again that my chance of coping effectively with life situations depends on self-awareness, values, skills, information and goals. Self-awareness is how I respond to situations. This helps me to build on my positive qualities and to be wary of any negative ones, which may get in the way. In truth, I always make conscious decision to enhance my life.

Values are defined by Tim (1983) as 'any kind of belief and obligation, anything preferred for any reason or for no apparent reason, any objective in the short or the long run, any idea or rule'. Values are beliefs held by a person of which he is not always aware. For this reason, it is always necessary to be aware of your values, examine them and also to accept the fact that our values may be different from others. This will help us in judging or criticising people. Our skills are our main resources which enable us to achieve our desired goals. Skills gained through experience, practice, education and training, are the only way to translate our values into action. Information or knowledge is necessary in our development and empowerment. Without information, the choices open to us are limited. Knowledge has great power. If a man is known by the company he keeps, so is his character reflected in the books he reads. J. Osward Sanders urges us to discriminate in our choice of books, to only read the best: that which invigorates our mission. Our reading should be regulated by who we are and what we intend to accomplish. For it is the outward expression of our inner hunger and aspiration.

Life that thrives requires an understanding of the long-term goals and objectives – where you want to go. Focus on a great goal and stop being worried about how you look, what others will think of you or whether you are going to fail. Losers are characterised by having few clearly stated goals other than self-pity, worries and frustration; they don't make their goals explicit. They have an inability to analyse situations, lack general competence and absence of personal responsibility. Setting goals is a means by which I take charge of my life. I take time to think about my values and the direction I would like my life to follow. I then make choices through reflection and prayer, followed by action. My goals are specific and realistic.

The power of language in empowerment

Language is the main medium of human communication whether in spoken or written form. Its use is empowering to both ourselves and the people with whom we are communicating. We can destroy the divine spirit which is in every human being with our tongue. As God created the world with words, with very little effort, we can either create or kill with words. 'All that it takes is either a kind or hard words'. One of the greatest merits a person can own is a benevolent eye – one that sees the good in all people – an eye that looks kindly on others and is not prepared to ruin someone else's reputation to gain the upper ground; the eye that avoids paying attention to hearsay and an eye that finds something in someone to compliment.

It is always advisable to use positive and active language. Positive words acknowledge your strengths and weaknesses while active words imply positive action rather than vague statements. If you fail to use words to define your own space and identity others will tend to define you by their own standard and thereby prompt you to evaluate yourself that way. They may even try to persuade you to conform to their demand.

In order to use words to help empower others, do not use jargons or complex terminologies. Focus on the words they are using so that you can tune in to what he is saying. Choose positive words. Avoid criticism and negativity. Criticism should always be given with extreme care and only when absolutely necessary and in a constructive way – through the use of positive and supporting words and phrases. Use open questions when appropriate. Such questions encourage people to take responsibility for their thoughts and actions. It also helps them to solve their problems through their own devices, set goals and work out an appropriate plan of action.

Stop gossiping

Rabbi Shmuley Boteach says that there is no more effective way to ruin another person's reputation than by gossiping about him, particularly if it is done cleverly, with wit and just a glimmer of truth. It is said that 'the gossip of two women will destroy two houses and that it speaks ill of all, and all of her'. When you talk about a person behind his back the victim has no way of responding, and if you are believed, his reputation suffers and his credibility dies; therefore gossiping is a murderous activity. All the more tragic is that the damage caused by gossip is irreversible. You cannot take your words back, or know how far they have spread. Gossip is cruel, evil and kills; that is why ruining someone's character and reputation in this way is called 'character assassination'. Before sitting down to gossip about people remember that, 'a person's reputation is as important as his life. His reputation dictates how he is received by society and his degree of professional success. When his reputation is ruined, it can be a permanent blow to his way of living and livelihood', writes Rabbi Shmuley Boteach. On the other side of the coin, those that gossip seldom come out on top: 'He who speaks much of others burns his tongue', for those who speak maliciously of others do soon hear bad things said of themselves. Avoid tale bearers, for he who chatters to you, will chatter of you; the dog that fetches will carry. Where there are no hearers, there would be no backbiters.

Personal development

Personal actualisation is the desire that every one has to become everything that they are capable of becoming. It means self-fulfilment and the need to reach full potential as a unique human being. Rich DeVos once wrote, 'If you have that flame of dream down inside you somewhere, thank God for it, and do something about it … ' We can build our lives if we assess our skills and qualities, consider our aims in life and set goals which will help us maximise our potential. This is personal development which continues throughout life.

There are many ideas surrounding personal development but I may briefly throw a light on that of Abraham Maslow's process of self-actualisation. According to Maslow, we all have an inbuilt need for development which occurs through the process of self-actualisation. The extent to which people are able to develop depends on certain needs being met and these needs form a hierarchy. Only when one level of need is satisfied can a higher one be developed. At the bottom of the hierarchy are the basics for survival. This is the need for food, drink, sexuality and sleep. Second is the need for safety and security in both the physical and economic sense. Third is the need for love and belonging. Fourthly is the need for self-esteem and self-worth. The fifth level is the need to know and understand the environment which consists of the curiosity and the search for meaning or purpose. Sixthly, progression can be made to aesthetic needs of beauty, symmetry and order. At the top of the hierarchy is the need for self-actualisation – the desire that every individual has 'to become everything that they are capable of becoming'. The needs are shown in the diagram below. As changes occur throughout life, however, the level of need motivating people's behaviour at any one time will alter.

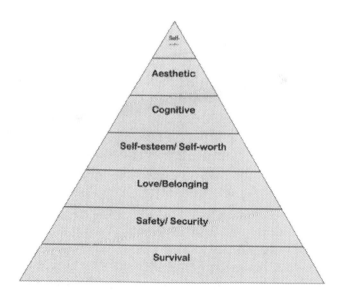

Self-actualisation

Steps to personal development

We can enhance our personal development by organising our time, producing a curriculum vitae (CV), undertaking a skills appraisal, looking at our transferable skills and overcoming barriers to learning a new skill. Drawing up a CV is not only necessary when applying for jobs. It also helps appraise the skills we have attained through education, training, employment, voluntary work and leisure activities.

Time keep on ticking

Think about these reflections on time, 'An inch of gold will not buy an inch of time', 'Time is money', 'He that has time, has life', 'Gain time, gain life'; 'Time undermines us', 'Time flies', 'Time has wings', 'Time flies without delays'. 'We must be very careful how we live—not as unwise but as wise, making the most of every opportunity, because the days are evil.' (Ephesians 5: 15-16) The best use of one's life is to spend it on something that will outlast it. Life's value is not its duration but its donation – not how long we live but how fully and how well. If you are careful about days, the years will take care of themselves. It is a mistake to say, 'I don't have the time' to accomplish a goal. We have the time to do the whole will of God for the rest of our lives. Our problem is not too little time, but making better use of the time we have.

We must 'redeem our time'. A carefully planned life is very important. We must carefully select priorities. We must thoughtfully weigh the value of different opportunities and responsibilities. If we want to excel, we must select and reject, then concentrate on the most important items. It is impossible to respond to every need.

11

THE FALLOW GROUND

Lord Mandelson rallied Labour troops with a stirring speech at the Labour Party Conference in Brighton, urging them not to surrender power meekly to the Conservatives. Fight 'like insurgents, not as incumbents' he told the conference. Complacency, our comfort zone, distractions, false beliefs and past failures are powerful evils that are fatal to success. We must at all cost not surrender to them. They will stagnate us in life.

Complacency is when an individual surrenders to an inner urge to take it easy. Colin Turner reckons that complacency is self-satisfaction in the belief that there is no point in finding out what you want; that it is the characteristic of classic low achievers that look for 'the easy life'; the sort that have no desire to excel because they are okay with mediocrity and being average. Even when things are handed to them on a plate they cannot be bothered to make use of opportunity, preferring instead to use most of life to distract others.

Colin Turner counsels that one thing that cripples and stunts our progress is 'our comfort zone'. It tames us to be comfortable with our circumstances and makes us very reluctant to break free from the status quo. It cripples us in our weaknesses, effectively taking our greatest aspirations and turning them into excuses for not bothering to aspire. Our 'comfort zone' gives us comforting reasons for why life didn't go the way it should, for why we experience failure. Think about this, 'those last few moments of sleep are delicious. It is dangerous to sleep when we should be working'. We are to utilise our energies and resources. Too much sleeping is laziness, which is a snare, as it turns us from our responsibilities and leads us to poverty. 'A little sleep, a little slumber, a little folding of the hands to rest – and poverty will come on you like a bandit and scarcity like an armed man' the Bible warns. (Proverbs 6:10-11)

Our 'comfort zone' is the trap of mediocrity, it is fatal to success. Diligence, on the other hand, is the mother of good fortune, a great teacher and makes an expert workman. 'No sweet without sweat.' 'No pains no gains.' Remember that the race is won by running.

A major determinant of your success is the ability to focus on your vision. Distraction is the enemy of progress. It is designed to test people to see if they really want what they want; if they really are following their heart; if they really are worthy of whatever it is. Distraction is planted along the pathway to our dreams and does anything it can to tempt us from being the individual God planned us to be. Tempting us off our path, temptation offers food, sex, fame, power, success (in any area other than that of our dream), recognition and easy money, literally anything to bait us away from our goal.

Leaving the pathway is always our choice, comments Colin Turner. We may choose to pursue what we want and follow the path to become a winner, or chase rats to become a loser. We must not lose our single mindedness. Keeping sight of your vision can be very difficult when there are so many distractions threatening to sidetrack us. Just as Eve lost her focus by listening to the serpent, we too can lose our focus by letting our lives become overcrowded and confused. Concentrate on keeping attitudes, actions and words focused on God. Do not let the negatives cause you to lose sight of the positives. Do not let potential difficulties blind you to God's power to help and His promise to guide. Distraction is time-wasting, energy-draining and frustrating.

Our currently held beliefs, whether good or bad, true or false, ideas we have uncritically accepted from others, or ideas we have repeated to ourselves or convinced ourselves as true, have an effect upon our behaviour. Belief is a powerful tool of behaviour and ability. A negative belief throws up a road block in our efforts to achieve the purpose in hand and holds us back in life. Replace the negative belief with a positive belief and it is like discovering a magic wand to make things happen. We are able to do surprising things only when we are convinced of our abilities, but within us is the power to do things we never dreamt possible. This power becomes available to us as soon as we de-hypnotise ourselves of the ideas 'I cannot', 'I am unworthy', 'I don't deserve it', and other self-limiting notions. Many beliefs and traditions are not bad in themselves. Certain beliefs can add richness and meaning to life. But we must not assume that because a belief or tradition has been practised for years, it should be elevated to a sacred standing. Any belief that is based on human ideas and experiences and discredits God is not the ideal solution to life's problems. God's principles never change, and his laws don't need additions. Our beliefs should help us to understand God's laws better and progress in life, they should not become laws in themselves. To resist heresy we must use the mind, keep our eyes on Christ and study God's Word.

Many people have memories of past failures; unpleasant and painful experiences which they constantly 'dig out'. It is good to remember our past mistakes or experiences to guide us in our future goals, for our errors, mistakes, failures and humiliations are necessary steps in the learning process, but they are a means to an end and not an end in themselves. If we consciously dwell upon our past failures, feel guilty about them, and keep on berating ourselves because of them, we make failure the ultimate goal in our memory. Condemning and torturing ourselves over past failures destroys our chances of happiness in the present, we may then live in bitterness and resentment. The minute we change our minds and stop giving power to the past, the past with its mistakes loses power over us. F. Meyers was right when he said that many people carried around within themselves talents, abilities and powers which are locked in, unused, merely because of memories of past failures.

John A. Schindler once said, 'Regardless of the omissions and commissions of the past, a person has to start in the present to acquire some maturity so that the future may be better than the past.' Present and future successes depend on learning new habits and finding other ways of looking at old problems. There is no future in digging into the past.

How do you control present thinking to produce contentment? Acknowledging sincere regret for any wrong doing or hurt caused, by giving apologies, accepting the circumstances that seem stacked against us, with determination, wisdom and hope in God, we can rise up again.

The glory of the power of God is upon us (Isaiah 60:1-2) because He wants us to be the lighthouse of the world and to operate in great fame and wealth. He wants us to step forward, to arise and shine. (Isaiah 60:1) Think about this, 'See darkness covers the earth and thick darkness is over the people, but the Lord rises upon you and His glory appears over you. Nations will come to your light and kings to the brightness of your dawn.' (Isaiah 60:2) 'You are the salt of the earth … you are the light of the world … let your light shine before men, that they may see your good deeds and praise your Father in heaven.' (Matthew 5:13-15) Many passages in the Scriptures point to God's desire to see our fruitfulness so that we can represent Him to the rest of the world. Forcefully forge ahead, without distraction, towards this purpose in your life. Develop the passion to do whatever it takes to succeed for complacency is fatal to success.

Growing up
A blossoming life always prioritises growth for which it pays the price. The man with a goal thinks like this: I have potential implanted within me by God. I shall find it and study it. I shall be committed to this goal, for my

commitment will determine how far I will go. In view of this, I shall invest my blood, sweat and tears to pursue my vision to excellence. This is a dream for my own life, and I am not working for anybody else. We need to take responsibility for our personal growth or transformation.

Growing up is not automatic, it takes personal commitment, writes Rick Warren. It involves moral endeavour and activity. We must want to grow, decide to grow, make an effort to grow, and persist in growing. We are not only to 'let go', we are also to 'put off' and 'put on' certain things, and this involves the definite activity of the renewed will, not the inevitable results of passive day dreaming about growth. We must change our thinking, recognise our weaknesses, make corrections and cultivate strength. We must clearly define our goals that will stretch, challenge and unify our life's activities. Ready to grasp the nettle of difficult situations and deal courageously with them, do not procrastinate hoping that problems will vanish with time. Do not sacrifice depth of vision for breadth of vision.

Trying to do anything without the necessary skills is like chopping wood with a dull axe. (Ecclesiastes 10:10) If you feel you lack formal skills, sharpen them with training and practice. Find the areas of your life where your 'axe' is dull, and cultivate your skills so that you can be more effective in what you do.

Everything has a beginning

Everything must have a beginning. The beginning of everything is the seed of it. Out of the seed comes the fruit: without the seed, there is no root and no fruit. Rivers need a spring. Every beginning is hard: the first step is the hardest; the greatest step is that taken out of the door. The beginning may be formless and empty. In the beginning, the world was a different place from our world of today. The nature of the beginning should not however scare you.

No matter how you find yourself, remember that now is the beginning of your life. It is not the end of your life. It is the beginning of a great thing, a future glory and honour. Let today be a dawn of a new day, a stir of hope, a beginning of imaginative visions for the future. No matter how dark your situation seems, God has a plan. Your end is certain. (Jeremiah 29:11) No matter how insignificant or useless you feel, God loves you and wants to use you in His plan. There is hope. Think about this; 'The Lord blessed the latter part of Job's life more than the first ...' (Job 42:12) 'There is a future for the man of peace.' (Psalm 37:37)

Good foundation

What is important is building a good foundation for life. If the beginning is good, the end must be perfect. A good beginning makes for a good end. An ill beginning makes for an ill end. Such a beginning and such an end well begun is half done. There is no good in building without a good foundation.

There are two ways to build: either upon sand (an unstable foundation) or upon a rock (a stable foundation). The best foundation of all for a building is bedrock. Other less stable layers such as gravel, sand, soil, clay and porous rock should be cut away so that a large structure can be built on bedrock. Perhaps people build houses without good foundations to save time and avoid the hard work of preparing a stone foundation, possibly because the waterfront scenery is more attractive or because beach houses have higher social status than cliff houses. Perhaps they want to join their friends who have already settled in sandy areas. Maybe they have not heard about the violent storms coming, or have discarded reports, or for some reason they think disaster can't happen to them. Whatever their reasons, those with no good foundation are short-sighted and will be sorry.

The foundations support the building. If it has good, deep and sure foundations, the building will stand, no matter what comes against it. If not, when troubles occur, the building will fall. (Luke 6: 46-49). When life is calm, our foundations don't seem to matter. But when crisis comes, our foundations are tested. Be sure your life is built on the solid foundation of knowing and trusting Jesus Christ.

Everything God created was good. In fact it was very good. (Genesis 1:10; 12; 18; 21; 25; 31) The Creation, as fashioned and ordered by God, had no lingering traces of disorder. God appraised whatever He made on the day and saw that it was good.

One step at a time

There is also this secret of life I have learnt from the Evolution theory or how God created heaven and earth 'One task at a time'. Many biologists now believe that there is sufficient evidence to suggest that evolution has followed a general course: Life began in water as a result of the reaction between chemicals in the early earth's atmosphere and oceans; the first life forms were unicells; they became more complex as cells acquired more and more organelles; simple multi-cellular organism evolved; they became more and more complex giving rise to plants and animals; some of these organisms colonised the land and the evolution of land animals, plants and fungi began.

We must shut the door of yesterday – the dead yesterday, shut the door of the future – the unborn tomorrows and live today to the full. The best possible way to prepare for tomorrow is to concentrate with all our intelligence, all our enthusiasms, on doing today's work superbly well. When we start the morning, there are hundreds of tasks we feel able to accomplish that day, but we must take them one at a time and let them pass through the day slowly and evenly.

Every day is a new life to a wise person. Do not put off living. Do not dream of some magical rose garden over the horizon instead of enjoying the roses that are blowing outside your windows today. Life is in the living, in the tissue of every day and hour. Today is God's gift to us. This is the day which the Lord has made; we must rejoice and be happy in it. Today is life, the very life of life. In its brief course lie all the verities and realities of our existence. Yesterday is but a dream. Tomorrow is only a vision. Today well-lived makes yesterday a dream of happiness and every tomorrow a vision of hope.

We must have no anxiety for tomorrow. By all means take thought of tomorrow, yes careful thought and planning and preparation, but have no anxiety.

Jump-start
I have also learnt that successful people do not wait for things to happen, but make them happen. They are self-starters, always on the look-out for improved methods and eager to test new ideas. The greatest achievements in history have come from people who took courageous and calculated risks. More failures come from an excess of caution than from bold experiments with new ideas. The 'frontiers of civilisation' are never advanced by cautious

people because most failures are the result of insufficient daring.

Guglielmo Marconi, the father of radio communications, studied under Professor Rosa and attended lectures by Professor Righi, both of whom were experimenting with Hertzian waves (as radio waves were called, after Heinrich Hertz, the first man to generate them). The young Marconi also began to experiment. He did not invent the instruments he used but improved on those of others. He was probably the first to realise that with the aid of a morse key the waves could be used to send messages. By this, Marconi transformed wireless waves from a scientific curiosity to an entirely new form of communication.

Read the biographies and autobiographies of successful people and you will discover that each of them have a common trait; they initiate. Many people are more gifted at conserving innovations than they are starting new ventures, for maintaining order rather than generating order. To reach heights in life, one must be venturesome as well as visionary. One must be ready to jump-start as well as hold speed. One should take calculated risks, always carefully, but reaching for what lies beyond. J. Oswald Sanders continues, 'We must either initiate plans for progress or recognise the worthy plans of others.' Remain in front and give guidance and direction to those behind.

Journey mapping

Nor is that all! Think about this, 'Jerry drove a car across the city of Turin to get to the airport. It was relatively easy, despite the fact that it was a new city for him and his Italian could be summed up in two words, 'Ciao' and 'Grazie', certainly not enough to ask for directions. His success was due to his map quite simply; he had a destination and the map to find where he was going. Without the destination, the map is useless; without the map the destination cannot be found. In business or in life it is exactly the same. First we need a goal (or destination) then a business plan (or a map) to chart the best way to reach our goal; on this route lies success.

For fulfilment in life, know what you want to accomplish. Know what action needs to be taken to achieve your goal and take responsibility for achieving it. God said, "Let there be light' and there was light'. God knew what He wanted and declared it. One that looks ahead and makes provision for the future thrives. Although the future can seldom be predicted, and factors beyond our control may interfere with the best laid plans, a clear vision is necessary or otherwise events are left to chance. Life should not pan out by chance! Organisation is the key. Planning minimises problems, and with the clarity of vision planning provides, you are well placed to take advantage of all opportunities that arise en route. Planning, therefore, requires conscious determination for a course of action;

the decisions entailed are based on purpose, knowledge and considered estimates. Any plan of action, defined in the light of our strengths and weaknesses and forces that may influence our destiny, solves problems relating to our purpose in life. Nobody plans to fail, they just fail to plan, don't let it happen to you!

Believe in yourself, believe you can make it

Finally believe in yourself and the fact that you can make it. Every man and woman is made in the image of God. Within each of us lies a fragment of the divine. The soul that we possess dwarfs by far any material achievement. God wants us to be confident. Nothing is more impressive than a man who believes in himself and radiates confidence.

True confidence comes from feeling special; from knowing that there is no individual quite like you. We must believe that we have something essential to contribute to this world. True confidence is an inner experience and is achieved when we feel good about our character and actions. It is attained when we bring meaning into our lives. Our outer actions must reflect our innermost convictions. In the words of Shmuley Boteach, 'People who have the most confidence are those whose lives have a purpose and a direction'. They are dignified people and walk with their heads held high because they feel confident about the direction of their lives.

Be natural, be yourself rather than relying on artificial enhancement. The harder you try to impress, the more unnatural you will become. Discover your unique gift and offer it to the world. Develop your mind and emotions. Think of great things you can do. Always remember that you have been made in the image of God.

Believe you can make it. The son of an African goat herder has become the most powerful man in the world although, initially, there were fears that racists would never have a black man in the White House. There is no doubt that around 50 years ago the black–American community was utterly despised and demeaned. But the stage was set for Barack Obama because he believed he could do it and chose his arrows with conviction and shot with precision.

Many people become weak at the knees when they face impossible assignments and, consequently, allow themselves to develop the habit of making excuses for not doing things. We can move a mountain with faith in God. 'If you have faith as small as a mustard seed … Nothing is impossible for you.' (Matthew 17:20)

Few of us believe we can move mountains in life and, as a result, not many of us do! Lack of faith is a negative power. When the mind doubts, the mind attracts reasons to support the doubts.

Faith works this way. The I-am-positive-I-can attitude generates the power, skill and energy required to move mountains. When you believe you can do it, the 'how' develops as you plan. On the other hand, believing the impossible is impossible will ensure you never discover the steps that lead to great heights.

The assurance of answered prayer does not mean that God is a dispensing machine into which a prayer is put and out of which comes the answer. The promise of answered prayer puts spiritual demands upon the person asking. When we ask God we must believe in Him and never doubt Him. (James 1:6-8) Each and every one of us must meet the conditions of answered prayer to get his prayer answered. Develop a whole-hearted attitude; an unquestioning committal to God and an unquestioning faith in whatever you are asking of Him. Have faith in God.

12

Man like me running away

'We need to think like insurgents, not incumbents' was Lord Mandelson's battle cry to the faithful at the Labour Party Conference in Brighton. 'The party will go into next years' general election as underdogs but victory is still possible. The election is up for grabs. That's what we're fighting for. We may be the underdogs but if we show people that we have not lost the fighting spirit and appetite for change that has defined by this party throughout its history then we can and will win.' Referring to his own comeback from two cabinet resignations he said; 'If I can come back, we can come back'. Quitting is an enemy of persistence. It weakens and stunts the progress of persistence.

My resolution!

I have experienced trials of many different kinds. My ministry has gone through the deadliest storms. I have read many books and literature on how to grow a big church, and have attended many church-growth conferences, yet my church is not a mega church, but I have made up my mind not to become weary and suffer an unconscious lapse into frustration and stress. Colonel Sanders of Kentucky Fried chicken fame has been my role model. He drove thousands of miles marketing his chicken recipe to restaurants all over the southern states of America. On several occasions, he slept in his car because he could not afford a motel room. He was rejected by nearly 500 places. Today there are thousands of Kentucky Fried Chicken franchises in hundreds of countries all over the world. 'Grain by grain, the hen fills her belly.' The Colonel's vision absorbed all his energy and he could not afford to let anything take his eyes off his goal.

We are faced with much competition and opposition and many challenges in life. Irrespective of the trials and challenges, dropping out is not the best action. Dropping out may mean we get some temporary relief because we have avoided the responsibility and pressures that were associated with success. In truth, drop-outs are not happy people. They wallow in low self-confidence, have a guilty conscience and lack self-respect. This is especially true if the endeavours in which we were engaged added up to a right and worthy cause and our lives turn out to be a failure. 'Bear and forbear' is a motto that has led many to victory. It takes a great deal of hard work and heartbreak to face life's challenges. Without the strength to stay in the race, we may drop out. But the end or the objective, the desire to accomplish something, justifies the effort and the endurance of hard work.

Symptoms of quitters

Napoleon Hill listed the sixteen symptoms of quitters, sixteen attributes of those that show a lack of persistence. Failure to recognise and clearly define exactly what you want; procrastination, with or without cause; lack of interest in acquiring specialised knowledge; indecision, the habit of 'passing the buck' on all occasions instead of facing issues squarely; the habit of relying upon alibis instead of creating definite plans for the solution of problems; self-satisfaction, a readiness to compromise on all occasions, rather than meet opposition and fight it; the habit of blaming others for your mistakes and accepting unfavourable circumstances as being unavoidable; a weakness of desire due to neglect in the choice of motives that impel action; a willingness to quit at the first sign of defeat; lack of an organised plan in writing where it may be analysed; the habit of neglecting to move on ideas or grasp opportunity when it presents itself; wishing instead of willing; a general absence of ambition to be, to do and to win; searching for short cuts to success and fear of criticism or failure to create plans and to put them unto action because of what people will think, do or say. 'Anyone who puts a hand to the plough and then looks back is not fit for the Kingdom of God.' (Luke 9:62) God wants total dedication, not half-hearted commitment. We must count the cost and be willing to abandon everything else for the sake of our vision

In this section I shall briefly throw a lucid light on four common subjects:

- Begging off
- Endurance
- Self-control
- Self-sacrifice

Begging off

We are prone to taking the course of least resistance, of escaping responsibility. There may be more troubles than gains when taking up one's duty but there seems to be more serious consequences such as unhappiness, loneliness or guilt, (Hebrews 12:25, 28) which makes begging off not the best way forward.

Remain committed to responsibility. (Psalm 15:4) Flee from the temptation of begging off from your responsibilities, whether due to a love of pleasure, love of an easy life or fear of other people. We are the steward of our capacities, powers and opportunities, and must be faithful to stewardship. (1Corinthians 4:1-2) Watch Tower magazine reported recently that more than 15,000 husbands and fathers were declared delinquents by New York City's Welfare Department. In the past few years, these men have failed to financially support their wives and children as ordered by the Family Court. Together they were in arrears of $26 million. There are many other examples of irresponsible, anti-social behaviour in society.

Endurance

Literally, endurance is a distasteful sound. It is a stubborn desire to live: surviving a long ordeal of scarcity out of a necessity and being rescued just in time. You may become so weak in the process that others need to feed and take care of you; you may not be able to help anyone else, suffering with determination and waiting for the end of the ordeal to come.

Endurance from the Christian perspective is quite different. We endure knowing God is on our side. We do not despair and starve as we go to our vision because we are nourished spiritually. Our focus on God and desire to encourage others, take our mind away from hardship. Knowing where we are going and why strengthens us with joy. Negative attitudes weaken endurance, especially when we have lost the initial love and joy in the task at hand, and begin to look upon the endeavour as burdensome. Our joy also weakens when we just hang on waiting for opportunity. It is a sign that we need to think seriously about refreshing our endurance.

At times, failure is simply a signal that it is time to change direction. If we keep hitting a wall, we must step back and look for a door. If we keep taking the same detour, maybe it is not a detour but the road we should be on. Stop banging on doors that are closed and walk through the one that God has opened for you. If you are working in an environment where you don't really fit it doesn't mean you have failed, it means you need the God-given courage to make some changes. Nevertheless, endurance is a quality. It gives life. (Luke 21:19)

Self-control

Today's motor cars have speeds of 180 mph and have the capacity of 35–300 horsepower. But if a vehicle's speed is not controlled, it is an instrument of death. We are endowed with similar strength (speed) and faculty – mental, emotional and physical. As free, moral and creative agents, we are capable of using our strength, our capacity, wrongly or correctly, wisely or unwisely, lovingly or un-lovingly. If not controlled, our faculties, like the motor car's can cause much harm. (Proverbs 25:28)

Self-control is restraint over one's own impulses, emotions or desires. It is the act of having one's faculties and energies, especially inclinations and emotions, under your control. Self-control is best exercised at times of temptation or pressure, when there is a danger of acting unwisely or selfishly or quitting. A recent report suggested that failure to exercise self-control accounted for the spread of venereal disease, many illegitimate births, widespread marital unhappiness, drunkenness, accidents, multiple murders and sins of all kinds.

God is our perfect example of self-control. He has unlimited powers, yet He exercises them only in just, wise and loving ways. 'He is long-suffering, slow to anger.' (Psalm 103:8) At no time throughout Jesus' ministry did He ever lose control. He never acted rashly. (1 Peter 2:23) He finished His course with the crown. Exercise self-control with food and drink, relationships, with pleasures and occupations and contend with Satan and his hordes of demons. The most powerful aid to help us through is the Word of God, prayer, the Holy Spirit and love. When we walk by spirit we shall carry out not fleshly desires. (Galatians 5:16; Zechariah 4:6)

Lot's wife failed to exercise self-control, for they were instructed not to look back as they fled the doomed city of Sodom, (Genesis 19:17, 26; Luke 17:32) but Lot's wife did look back, and this led to her destruction. In the long run, the benefits and rewards of self-control greatly outweigh the effort in exercising it.

- Self-control makes for a healthy body and mind. Health is the reward of temperance. To live with a settled temper means long life.
- Self-control commands self-respect. (1 Peter 3:16) We may not be able

to keep people from slandering us but as long as we do what is right, accusations will be empty and embarrass only the perpetrators. Self-control keeps our conduct above criticism.

- Self-control keeps us from following 'after the crowd for evil ends'. (Exodus 23:2) With moral restraint, we can withstand the pressure of the crowd to sway our decision about a person; to let the fairness God shows guide our judgment.
- Self-control aids us in bearing the other fruits of the Holy Spirit. We cannot have joy, peace, patience, kindness, goodness, humility and faith unless we are disciplined of mind, heart and body.
- Our self-control blesses others, for it keeps us from making others stumble. By exercising self-control we set a good example and improve all our relationships.

Lack of self-control started the human race on the road to sin and death and has caused many a misery since. Checking your mental, physical and spiritual powers is never in vain. Temper passion and social excess. Learn to control yourself in a way that is holy and honourable and not powered by passionate lust. (1 Thessalonians 4:4-5) Learn to make level paths for the feet so that the lame may not be disabled but rather are healed.

Self-sacrifice

Sergeant Lockett, 29, of the Second Battalion Mercian Regiment, was awarded the Military Cross for his part in rescuing colleagues during a Taliban ambush in 2007. Military leaders praised his 'selfless commitment and unshakable bravery', for he drew enemy fire to rescue his comrades. Lockett was nearing the end of his third tour when he died.

We are becoming more and more self-indulgent and materialistic. (2 Timothy 3:1-5) If we want things to be different, there is a need to revive that spirit of self-sacrifice as taught by Jesus Christ (Luke 9:23-26) and demonstrated by the actions of Sergeant Lockett of Dundee. Watch Tower magazine defines self-sacrifice as giving up things, to some extent relating to the sacrifice of material things that constitute an attraction to the flesh, and which stand in the way of unhindered service to God. Some of these material attractions or fleshly desires may lead to over-indulgence, the sinful or fallen flesh, something condemned in God's Word or at least strongly counselled against. We must be able to evaluate and decide what is truly worthwhile and what is really beneficial. (Matthew 24:38-39) See life in its true light: consider what is being given up now as compared to the reward that is to be won. (Philippians 3:8; Genesis 25:29-34)

Tempting though it is to find excuses not to make changes where it will cause us to stand out, nevertheless, we should seize the opportunity to stand up uncompromisingly for the truth no matter what others may think or say. Be willing to pay a high price for something you value. If this present life is most important to us, we will do everything we can to protect it. We will not want to do anything that might endanger our safety, health or comfort. In the same way, if Christ is most important, we may risk death but not fear it in the knowledge that Jesus will raise us to eternal life. We shall not use our life for our own pleasure.

Developing persistence

Napoleon Hill has identified four simple steps that can lead us to a similar persistence essential for success in all walks of life. First, you need a definite purpose backed by a burning desire for its fulfilment. Knowing what you want forces you to surmount many difficulties. Second, just completing something by doing it is 100 per cent better than doing well something you never even start. Third, there should be a definite plan expressed in continuous actions. Organised plans, even though they may be weak or entirely impractical encourage persistence. Fourth, close your mind tightly against all negative and discouraging influences and suggestions and associate with people who will encourage you to follow through with both the plan and purpose. Avoid distractions. (Proverbs 4:27) and remain focussed on the task at hand and the promise of blessing, or the benefit of the success, of the endeavour to come.

One way to endure is to plan ahead. Determine the viability of the objective, is it a worthy cause? Carefully examine the validity of the means or the method to achieve the goal, how honest or just is the means to the end? Get the right view of endurance. 'He conquers who endures.' Firmly make up your mind to go ahead (Luke 14:28-38) and, having set the course, plug into your source of strength for stability in facing obstacles, and finish your course of action. There is always the need to evaluate and monitor your plan to ensure that in pursuing your goal you are not on a circuitous or drifting route but on a direct course towards your goal. (2 Corinthians 13:5)

Trials in life serve to sift the winners from the losers. When pressured to give up and turn your back on your purpose, do not do it. Always remember the benefit of standing firm and continue to pursue your goal to completion. Those who endure to the end will be saved. (Matthew 24:13) 'Feather by feather, the goose is plucked.' 'The best things are hard to come by.' 'The best fish swim near the bottom.' Finishing counts! Life, like every race, has its start and its finish, writes Dennis Burke. Though the start is certainly important, it is how you finish that counts. Many have finished their race strong. By faith they have refused to be governed by the moment that pressured their flesh but held on to their hope of better things ahead. (James 5:10-11)

After hard work and sacrifice, our effectiveness and credibility still come down to our daily decisions to let faith, hope and love rule. Job had staying power. He stayed the course and God brought it all together for him. God is always at work to bring it all together for us because he has not only called us to be his chosen and special people, but also cares about the details of our life. Hebrews (12:2) encourages us to keep our eyes on Jesus and God's Word to finish the race. We must keep our prayer-life fresh and spiritual being strong. Our faith will honour God, and in the process, we will be blessed and bring God's blessing to other people. (Revelations 3:10) Single-mindedness is a quality anyone who wishes to finish the course needs. Paul was a single-minded person. No wonder he was the greatest missionary who has ever-lived. God is looking for more people who will focus on that one great task he has given them to do. Always remember the words of Usain Bolt, '... with the 200 metres heats to come tomorrow, there will be no partying for me ...' and he finished the race with joy. What can't be cured must be endured

13

THE THREE BASIC HUMAN NEEDS

We are made to fulfil threefold aspiration:

- Self-esteem
- Relationship
- Transcendence.

Everything essential to life is contained in these three basic human longings. Our heart is restless without them. There is a hunger in the human heart which none but we, our neighbour and God can quench.

Self-esteem is basic to human survival. It means dignity, worth, value, respect and recognition placed on us. We have self-worth, if we think that we matter or we value ourselves as people. The value placed on us influences our personal happiness and establishes the boundaries of our accomplishments and fulfilment. If we have a bad self-image, we cannot escape from negative attitudes and ideas we have about ourselves. If we live with these, three things tend to happen. We lack confidence in ourselves. We are unable to discover our purpose in life. We get a sense of rejection, failure and insecurity. Many of our social problems today can arise from bad self-image.

All people have been made together. We have been made into a corporate relationship with other human beings. To live means to be part of a fellowship or a relationship and to support it loyally. Life without a relationship is like television without an aerial. You cannot live without and not enter into some sort of relationship. This is as ridiculous as saying, 'You can be a good footballer, but never join a team. A footballer is one who plays in a team'. Life knows nothing of solitary life. Growth, happiness, accomplishment and fulfilment can only be achieved through social relationships.

We are created to live in a relationship with God. Without that relationship there will always be a hunger, emptiness, a feeling that something is missing. For all the advances of science, there remains deep in the soul, a persistent and unconscious anxiety that something is missing, some ingredient that makes life worth living. From ancient times, man has been longing for transcendence. He has sought it through drugs, occultism, environment, sex and yoga. The spread of the New Age Movement, Pentecostalism, charismatic movements and other expressions of religion explains the dimension of man's desire to reach out for God.

Self-esteem

In the mid-19th century the Austrian monk, Gregor Mendel, was experimenting with sweet peas in his garden and made the initial discovery from which the modern science of genetics developed. In seeds from parent plants he discovered a large number of different factors, now known as genes, which he found always worked by a certain set of rules to control the appearance of the plant that would grow from the seed. Before long it was found that these rules, now called Mendelian Laws (laws of inheritance), were the same for every plant and animal, including human beings. This means that every living plant and animal reproduces its own kind of species, and no other.

Kenneth and Valerie McLeish note that on all previous days of Creation, God merely acted, bringing things into being by commanding their existence. By contrast, before the final act He announced His purpose and made it clear that He envisaged the human race as superior to all other living things, made in His own likeness and having a relationship with Him that no other species shares. Our reason, creativity, speech, self-determination and character – our entire self – reflects the image of God. Knowing that we are made in God's image and thus share many of His characteristics provides a solid basis for self-worth. We know God is the all-wise, all-powerful and all-knowing creator, and made us in His likeness, so we would not turn out to be inferior products. Our self-worth is not based on possessions, achievements, physical attractions or public acclaim, but on being made in God's image. For this reason, we must feel positive about ourselves.

God sees us as people of whom and through whom He can do great works. He sees us as already serene, confident and cheerful. He sees us not as pathetic victims of life, but as masters in the art of living, not seeking sympathy but imparting help to others.

Self-esteem amounts to the significance or value we feel is placed on us; it is a favourable, commendable, promising and suitable opinion of ourselves. The value placed on us influences our personal happiness and establishes the boundaries of our accomplishments and fulfilment. God made us and He knew us even before we were born. We must praise God because we are fearfully and wonderfully made. God's works are wonderful. (Psalm 139:14) There never was and never will be another person quite like us. We have been made and shaped by God for success irrespective of our circumstances and strengths. We are special in His sight.

Michael Marnu

The key to a better life

Self-image is your own perception of the sort of person you are. It is built up from your own beliefs about yourself – experiences, successes and failures. It is a key to living a better life because your actions, feelings, behaviour and abilities are always consistent with it. You 'act like' the sort of person you perceive yourself to be. If you perceive yourself to be a failure type of person, you will find some way to fail, in spite of all the opportunities that may come your way.

To a person with low esteem, almost anything can become a threat. When self-esteem is at a high level, people are easy to get along with. They are cheerful, generous, tolerant, willing to listen to others' ideas. To really 'live' you must be yourself and find yourself acceptable. You must have a self-trust and believe in, not feel ashamed of yourself; one must feel free to express oneself creatively. Your self-perception must therefore grow and improve with the renewal of your mind. Once self-perception is changed, other things consistent with your new self-perception are easily accomplished.

Think about this, 'An animal's 'animal-ness' is in itself, likewise your humanity depends for its existence upon God. For this reason, we cannot exist independently of God. We may want to live independently of God but we may bring disaster upon ourselves, as seen in the life of Adam. (Genesis 2:8-17; Genesis 3:1-24) 'No branch can bear fruit by itself; it must remain in the vine'. (John 15: 1-8)

Moving forward

Do you at times feel hesitant and lacking in confidence, wanting to make changes and to feel happier, but not knowing how? Below are some boosters as suggested by Patricia Cleghorn in The Secrets of Self-esteem.

'On a daily basis, stop criticizing yourself. Practice the three A's of self-esteem building; Appreciate yourself; Accept yourself; Approve yourself. Notice thoughts that are unhelpful: 'I will never get this done'; 'I cannot handle this'; 'I am not good enough' <u>and change them to</u> 'I am getting everything done'; 'I can handle this'; 'I am more than good enough'. Add good feelings to your self-esteem thoughts so that you immediately feel confident and successful. Imagine putting repetitive worries about the future and the past into a box and see them disappearing from your mind. Then you will feel free to take any action that is appropriate. Stop blaming yourself and others. When faced with unexpected change, relax and trust yourself to cope. Then you can more easily see what you need to do. Look for ways you can treat yourself better. Especially when you are under pressure, be extra kind to yourself and do things you enjoy. Relax for a few minutes daily. Listen to your personal intuition. You can ask yourself about any situation, 'What do I need to know? What do I need to do?

The answers can come either now or later. Listen to your personal intuition to guide you throughout the day. You are important, what you want is important. Where you are going is important. Dream, visualise, clarify. Listen to your personal intuition which has been refined by the Holy Spirit, to set goals in easy stages and take action. Always remember, you are special, your life is precious!'

Just for today

There are days when the last thing we want to do is rejoice. Our mood is down, our situation is out of hand, and our sorrow or guilt is overwhelming. No matter how low we feel, we must always be honest with God and praise Him in all things and at all times. (1 Thessalonians 5:16-18) As you sing praises unto God, He will give you a reason to rejoice. He has given you this day to live. Be glad. You may use Dale Carnegie's 10 Principles for making the best of the day to brighten this day.

'Just for today, I will be happy. Happiness is from within. It is not a matter of externals. [People] are about as happy as they make up their mind to be. Just for today, I will try to adjust myself to what is, and not try to adjust everything to my own desires. I will take my family, my business, my luck as they come and fit myself to them. Just for today, I will take care of my body. I will exercise it, care for it, nourish it, not abuse it nor neglect it, so that it will be a perfect machine for my bidding. Just for today, I will try to strengthen my mind. I will learn something useful. I will not be a mental loafer. I will read something that requires effort, thought and concentration. Just for today, I will exercise my soul. I will do somebody a good turn. Just for today, I will be agreeable. I will look as well as I can, dress as becomingly as possible, talk low, act courteously, be liberal with praise, criticise not at all, nor find fault with anything and not try to regulate nor improve anyone. Just for today, I will try to live through this day only, not to tackle my whole life problem at once. Just for today, I will have a programme. I will write down what I expect to do every hour. I may not follow it exactly, but I will have it. It will eliminate two pests: hurrying and indecision. Just for today, I will be unafraid especially to be happy, to enjoy what is beautiful, to love and to believe that those I love, love me.'

How do you carry yourself?

The boss of Britain's biggest driving school has dodged a car ban despite stacking up 17 points on his licence. He refused to reveal who was driving the car and copped six points on top of the 11 he already had. Normally 12 points means an automatic ban. An insider of the company, which coaches 170,000 people a year said, 'It is incredibly embarrassing teaching learners to obey rules if our driving force is a serious offender'. The head of the Driving Instructors Association said: 'I am amazed he has maintained his position as head of the company'.

Personality is all about how we project ourselves, how we cause other people to react to us. Our core beliefs, values, long-term goals and the degree to which we are sensitive to others, are all subsumed within the fabric of our character. Our character manifests itself in all our deeds. While we may well have a decent character, if we fail to demonstrate it with good deeds, we may easily earn a bad reputation. Wake up to the responsibility of working on your character and cultivate a reputation to match it! Strive to become trustworthy, reliable and straightforward in all your dealings. Our generation is marred by mistrust; take it as a wake-up call.

To live in God's presence, we must be honest. (Psalm 24:3-4) God expects honesty from us, (Proverbs 16:11) and He blesses us when we are more concerned about treating others fairly than we are about how much we will gain for ourselves. (Deuteronomy 25: 13-15) In all deeds remember that honesty demonstrates a character of quality; 'a good name is better than fine perfume.'

Superiority and inferiority complex

In our daily lives, there are two complexes we must avoid: superiority and inferiority complexes. Rakesh Ramachandran has observed that lack of recognition and a greater inferiority complex leads to a greater depressive time which was not noticeable as it was an early stage of personality development. It is true that love is a deciding factor in life which is the secret of all success. Due to the inferiority complex developed in the mind there is a development of superiority complex. This is a clever play by the mind to ensure the survival of the organism.

The inferiority complex develops due to a lack of recognition and love during the early stages of life where the actual development of the personality takes place. The lack of love and recognition creates a vacuum in the personality which is recognised by the subconscious mind. This leads to the subsequent development of a superiority complex, as a total inferior feeling in the mind will lead to the total death of the mind. This leads to a complex situation of mental agony and suppression of feelings and finally finds a way out as a superiority complex. He went further to explain that superiority complex is a game developed by the subconscious mind to hide its own inferior feelings. Without this superiority complex the mind would crumble under its own inertia. For survival the mind develops a superiority complex so that the mind can cling on to something for its survival.

At some point survival alone does not help a mind and it needs a triumph in life as well and that is when it becomes aware of this superiority complex in itself. He then suggested that since the superiority complex has developed due to the rise of an inferiority complex, the complete removal of the superiority complex is possible only by the removal of the inferiority complex as well. This is because the natural personality is devoid of these complexes

Inferiority Complex

Think about this, 'Janet dated Frank for more than six months. He regaled her with stories of the success of his automobile business. Although he never spent much money on her, he attributed this to the huge outlay of investment he was making to expand his business more rapidly. They got engaged and were happy. On the day of the wedding, Frank received a call from Janet that saddened him. Janet had called off the wedding. The whole story about his automobile business was false. He lied to her. Janet said that she couldn't care less whether or not he had money.

I believe that inferiority complex is a disorder arising from the conflict between the desire to be noticed and the fear of being humiliated. In an ordinary sense it is a feeling of inadequacy or insignificance. It has been observed that at least 95 per cent of people have their lives blighted by feelings of inferiority to some extent, and that this feeling of inferiority comes about because we compare ourselves unfavourably with others. We judge ourselves, and measure ourselves against another individual's 'norm'. We wish or desire to be like somebody or be like everybody else. Invariably everyone is unique and special. It is important to realise that, as people, we are all different. We are born with our own set of strengths and weaknesses, and our personal circumstances, intelligence, nationality, economic circumstances, environment and parentage have moulded us as individuals. If we fail to see the innate differences in others and accept ourselves as we are, we may think we are not like others and, therefore, are slightly irregular.

Are you kept down with by an inferiority complex? Remember that the only way to cure an inferiority complex is to build an inner security, one which is found through finding and being you. Work on your confidence, remembering always that confidence is not something that can be learned like a set of rules, however, it can be improved with positive thought. It comes from feelings of well-being, belief in your own ability, skills and experience. It can be eroded by fear. Gain control of yourself. Do not be a complainer. Learn to relax. Boost your own morale. Learn to channel nerves and tension positively.

Notwithstanding these, the truth is that our worth is not based on possessions, achievements, physical attractions or public acclaim but being made in God's image. For this reason, we must feel positive about ourselves. God sees us as people of whom and through whom he can do great works. He sees us as already serene, confident and cheerful. He sees us not as pathetic victims of life, but masters of the art of living, not wanting sympathy but imparting help to others. Remember always that Jesus, the Son of God, came to the earth knowing that many people are filled with self-hatred, think badly of themselves; harbour bitterness or resentment against God for making them the way they were. He came to restore to man what has been lost. Listen to Him, 'Come to me, all you who labour and are heavy laden and I will give you rest...' (Matthew 11:28) He is our source of hope in times of crisis. He came that we may have life, and have it to the full. (John10:10)

14

RELATIONSHIP

As a recap, all people have been made together. We have been made into a corporate relationship with other human beings. To live means to be part of a fellowship or a relationship and to support it loyally. Life without a relationship is like television without an aerial. You cannot live without and not enter into some sort of relationship. This is ridiculous as saying, 'You can be a good footballer, but never join a team. A footballer is one who plays in a team'. Life knows nothing of solitary life. Growth, happiness, accomplishment and fulfilment can only be achieved through social relationships.

Enriching your relationships
There was a story of Mimmi who went out with a beautiful girl on four dates. In that time she

criticised everything about him, from the tie he wore to the restaurant he chose, to the cologne he splashed on. When asked for a fifth date, he rejected the offer and replied, 'Margaret, you know how much I love you and how I will always be there for you. But that's exactly why I don't understand why you always belittle me'.

To be able to get along with somebody in a relationship, we need to remember three things:

- Understand that people are not alike
- Do not judge others and
- Make a real commitment.

It is important to realise that we are all different. We were born with our own set of strengths and weaknesses and our circumstances, intelligence, nationality, economic situation, environment and parentage have moulded us as individuals. If we cannot see the innate differences in others and accept them as they are, we will think anyone who is not like us is slightly irregular. Secondly, remember not to judge your neighbour. Each of us tries to remake the other in a relationship; realise that someone could be different and still not be wrong. Let's not be of the type who is always right and knows everything. Instead of trying to shape one another in a relationship, strive to encourage, love and help one another. Lastly, a fruitful relationship requires commitment from all involved parties. A relationship can only exist when all those involved are functioning as they should be; when each person gives priority to sustaining the relationship and pays the sum on the price tag for its growth. Those who put in the most get the most out of the commitment.

Love is the big gun of life

Experience is the best teacher. I have learnt this over and over again throughout my life. 'Love is the big gun of life.' It is wonderful to remind one that we all belong, by virtue of our being human, to one big family. God has made us together. The world and every good deed are useless without love. Knowing all, moving mountains, giving all we have to the poor, and even dying for our faith, mean nothing if we do not have love. Love is the big gun of life; among peace conferences or terrorism, love is what counts. Love is the cement that holds the world and families together.

We need to work at love, demonstrate it by acts of thoughtfulness, encouragement and unselfishness. We should watch not only our actions but also our reactions to what others do or say. Be patient with other's faults, for a forgiving spirit is what we must have in our hearts even before the person who has wronged us says he is sorry. Real love is based on the deliberate choice of the one who loves rather than the worthiness of the one who is loved, which goes against natural human inclination, for real love is a giving, selfless, expect-nothing-in-return kind of love. Love does not seek its own but compels us to set aside our own plans, agendas and entitlements for the good of another. It centres upon determining what is best for another person and then doing it. 'Because love covers over a multitude of sins.' (1 Peter 4:8)

We must accept that other people's rights are our responsibility. We are our brother's keeper, because we are in the same human family and so are related to one another and are responsible for one another. Do not sweep away your duty to your neighbour to expand your own rights; the continual assertion of rights against another person encourages selfishness and conflict. Think about this. Love is determined to seek the other's best. This is love in practice.

Attitude within relationships

Senior ministers rallied around the UK's beleaguered prime minister amidst news his poll ratings had slumped still further. The culture minister defended the PM claiming his leader's 'big brain' would steer the country through recession. Another minister commented that the PM is the right leader for the party and the country, and lamented the way people consistently underestimated him to the detriment of the nation. The minister's comments came as the party's support dwindled to 23 per cent. These comments testify to the notion that positive attitudes breathe life, peace and harmony into relationships while negative ones kill it and bring upheaval and disharmony.

We should, therefore, love one another, encourage one another, spur one another on towards love and good deeds, build one another up, edify one another, admonish one another, instruct one another, serve one another, bear one another, forgive one another, be kind to one another, be compassionate to one another, be devoted to one another, honour one another, live in harmony with one another, be sympathetic with one another, be gentle with one another, be patient with one another, accept one another, submit to one another, clothe ourselves with humility towards one another, teach one another, live at peace with one another, confess our mistakes and sins to one another, pray for one another, offer hospitality to one another, greet one another, have fellowship with one another, agree with one another and carry one another's burdens.

Conversely, there are eight things that cool a relationship; avoid doing these things to others. Do not bite or devour one another, do not provoke or envy one another, do not hate one another and do not judge one another. Do not lie to one another, do not slander or speak evil about one another, do not grumble about one another and do not go to law against one another.

If you want to live in harmony with others, remember the key to a good attitude lies with the Holy Spirit; allow Him to control your mind. When we give God control over our lives He bestows on us His attitude and His ways. (Romans 8:6; Romans 12:2) God has selfless, sacrificial and unconditional love for us and wants us to have the same love for others. 'Greater love has no man, than a man lay down his life for his friends.' (John 15:13) Jesus is the source of love for a neighbour. In view of this, unless the love of Jesus filters into society it will be impossible for humanity by its own strength and volition to move from selfish competition to loving cooperation.

Tissues of relationship

I wish to conclude this chapter by sharing with you the fourteen tissues of relationships, what makes relationships last. These revolve around philosophies, beliefs, values and character traits that have proven to be most sustaining and valuable in relationship.

- Seeing someone as 'nobody repels him'.

Often we treat a well-dressed, impressive-looking, rich person better than someone who looks shabby and poor. We do this because we would rather identify with successful people than with apparent failures.

God views all people as equals, and if He favours the poor and powerless we should follow His example and treat all people as we would want to be treated. By treating all people as important we disregard what we think they are, our prejudiced ideas and knowledge about them, and treat them as unique individuals, respecting their viewpoints and feelings and acknowledging their relevance. By noticing other people and paying them attention, we make them feel important and good about themselves: when you 'notice' somebody, you are paying him a compliment and your compliment immediately boosts the other person's morale, making him more friendly and cooperative. Spending time incorporating new people into your life is a positive assertion of faith.

Do not lord over people, attempting to grow your own self-importance while making others feel small; respect people and make them feel that they belong. Do not attempt to win all the little battles. Criticise or correct people in a positive way; building on the strengths of their endeavours. Finally, do not underestimate the importance of small courtesies and polite behaviour, for by these small things we acknowledge the importance of others. Treat family members, friends, colleagues and fellow inmates with the same courtesy you would give a stranger. Everybody is hungry for significance. See somebody as nobody and you will repel him. Remember always that it takes all sorts to make a world.

- The Mirror

Our own attitudes are reflected back to us when we are dealing with people, almost as if we were stood in front of a mirror. Confidence breeds confidence, and just as enthusiasm is catching, so too is indifference. If we are treated discourteously, maybe it is because we ask for it. You can alter someone's emotional response to you depending on how you initiate the meeting. Just as a soft answer turns away wrath, if we adopt harsh tones we can expect conflict, so adopt the attitude you wish the other person to express.

How we project ourselves reflects back on us. No one likes a failure, but if you act as if you don't know where you are going, then you are writing exactly that history. Hold your head up and demonstrate to others that you are walking confidently in the direction of 'somewhere important to go'. If we believe in ourselves and respect others, others will believe in us and recognise us.

Although sometimes, despite our labours and good works, we witness no tangible results or receive any thanks, have faith that in due time we will reap a harvest of blessing. If we live only to please our selfish desires we will reap only sorrow and evil but if we live to please God we shall reap joy and everlasting life. There are consequences to every action, so you reap what you sow; all actions get results. Adopting a lifestyle that when bounced back to us puts laughter on our lips is imperative therefore. Remember always that evil deeds are like perfume, difficult to hide.

- Little things give us away

According to Les Giblin our physical actions express our mental attitudes. Little things, such as how we walk, our handshake and the tone of our voice, give us away. For example, timid people are easily identified by the way they walk with head and eyes downcast, shoulders bent and dropped. When it comes to hand-shaking, confident people shake hands firmly with just a little squeeze, while the discouraged straddle two extremes, the limp, dish-rag type of handshake or the bone-crusher type. Confident people communicate effectively, expressing hope and courage while those who lack confidence are often pessimists, moaning and constantly blaming others. Initially, anyway, appearance is an effective way of influencing people.

Regrettably, though, when people are judged by outward appearance only, outstanding individuals are overlooked if they do not hold the physical qualities currently admired in society. But appearance alone does not reveal your true value. God judges by faith and character, for He can see inside. While not obsessed by every detail of our behaviour, neither should we be unconcerned and forget to be courteous and personable. While personal hygiene, neatness and grooming are also important in a person's attitude an inner spirit is where true beauty begins. Remember always that you can't tell a book by its cover.

- Impressions

'Follow my example, as I have followed the example of Christ', Paul instructed a group of new believers who did not know much above the life and ministry of Jesus Christ, and could not be asked to imitate Him according to the Gospel because it had not been written at the time. Paul saw that the best way to direct the new believers to Christ was to point them in the direction of the Christians he trusted. Paul had been in Corinth for almost two years and built up a relationship of trust with many of the new believers.

How we are accepted by others is largely up to us, for every time you have dealings with people you set the stage. Your first words, actions and attitudes sound a keynote for the entire encounter; first meetings are likely to leave a lasting impression that will determine how that person regards you for the rest of your association. None of us are wholly bad or wholly good, nor are we the same person to everyone we meet. Initial impressions are engraved on the minds of all parties, but the personality we present is what they bring out in us and is likewise dependent on what we bring out in them. If we want people to take us seriously we must sound the keynote in the first seconds of meeting them. Considering that at first we are evaluated on the opinions we hold about life – for example religion, national, international, local or familial politics – avoid negative opinions that might create a bad and lasting impression, and do not be a sore-headed, for no one wants to know or work with a moaner or a chronic complainer. In all this, do not strive so hard at making a good impression so that you forget to let the other person know they are making good impression on you!

- The power of praise

Words of praise, writes Charles Fillmore, expand and set free individuals and in every way radiate energy. You can praise a weak body into strength, a fearful heart into peace and trust, shattered nerves into poise and power, a failing business into prosperity and success, and need and insufficiency into supply and support.

The whole of creation responds to praise. People from all walks of life are hungry for praise and appreciation; it is the one thing people desire. Praise is like injecting life into a person; give him praise and he will in turn give you what you want. It was for this reason that King David, the man of God's heart, regularly appointed singers and musicians to minister before the ark, to compose, and give thanks and praise to God. They ministered continually, morning and evening, during David's life. (1 Chronicle 16:4) The basis for his praise was to declare God's character and attributes in the presence of others. When we recognise and affirm God's goodness we are holding up His perfect, moral nature for all to see.

Praise benefits us because it takes our minds off our own problems and needs and focuses on God's power, mercy, majesty and love. It also involves ascribing glory to God, and while doing so, boosts our own happiness. Deliberately looking for good things to compliment in others has a positive effect on us. It takes our mind off our own needs, making us less self-conscious, less self-righteous, tolerant and understanding, and, thereby, cures many worries, fears and anxieties. Praising other people helps us to stop finding fault with them and, as we begin to change our opinion about them, we focus on the good in people and realise that no one is perfect and that there is some good in everyone. Remember always to praise youth and it will prosper

- Thank you

Learn how to say 'thank you' to people. Saying 'thank you' releases energy in people if it is sincere. Speak praise boldly, do not mumble. When we compliment a person on a specific thing they have done, they feel good about themselves and what they have done, which motivates them to do more of the same. Praise inflates the ego. Every time we say the words 'thank you', and mean it, we are giving the other person credit – praising them for having done something we appreciate. When we demonstrate our appreciation, rather than taking good works for granted, it makes them want to do still more for us.

Work at thanking people; deliberately look for things to thank people for. Praise is often more powerful when the other person does not expect it, so thanking people when they least expect it can be very effective. Do not wait until someone does something momentous or unusual before you offer praise.

No matter how difficult your life's journey, you can always count your blessings or someone's glorious deed – past, present and future. King David in the Old Testament was popular for singing out praises to God. He was overwhelmed by what God had done. He believed that God was great and could not help telling others about Him. His heart was full of appreciation for what God had done. It is easy to complain about life, but David found plenty for which to praise God. (Psalm 103:1-22). Remember always that true praise roots and spreads.

- Deadly sin in conversation

Wilfred Frank, Editorial Director of Your life magazine, made a study of thousands of successful men and women, looking for a common denominator. He found that the one thing they owned in common was a skill with words. Words have the power of life and death. There is a deadly sin in conversation which must be avoided at all costs, writes Les Giblin. This is the temptation to talk about you to impress the other person. If the sole intention is to inflate your own ego expect to get nothing out of the conversation. The time to talk briefly about 'you' is when you are invited to tell someone about yourself.

You can talk your way to success when you use 'happy talk' as much as possible. No one likes to sit down and listen to a 'prophet of doom'. People don't like to hear bad news, so to go on endlessly about your 'bad times' is never anything but boring. Eliminate kidding and teasing from your conversation and leave sarcasm behind as it makes people feel small and defensive. In volatile situations, a soft answer is akin to throwing water over a flame and often defuses potentially explosive situations. Conversely, a raised voice and harsh words almost always trigger an angry response. To turn away wrath and seek peace, choose gentle words. (Proverbs 15:1) You can help free people from their blanket of burden by kind words, listening and offering wise encouragement. (Proverbs 12:25) Remember always that good news may be told at any time, but ill in the morning.

- Attracting people

The main reason for the footballer, Toure's, move from City to Eastlands was not financial but due to the fact that he knew he would be appreciated at the new club. He vowed to reward City for showing faith in him. Listen to him: 'They have showed they really want me and I'm very happy. I've always said when you love a woman and she gives you love back, you're really happy.' writes a tabloid. Our souls are hungry and thirsty for three basic emotional-spiritual foods. We are drawn, therefore, to people who are able to nourish us, and choose our friends consciously or unconsciously because they satisfy our three basic hungers.

First is acceptance – the ability to welcome people as they are. Let people be themselves. No one likes a moaner or someone who nags all the time or complains a lot and scolds people. The critical, fault-finding type who hones in on where others fall short, and can usually also suggest a remedy, does not make a good friend. The more we set rigid personal standards about how we believe others should act, the more we drive them away. Second is approval – to find something to approve of in everyone. It may be something small or insignificant but we all want somebody to find something positive in us. Being positive, you are always on the look out for something in someone about which you can approve, rather than negatively finding fault in others. When others realise the taste of our genuine approval their behaviour changes towards us, and other areas of their life – and ours– are improved. Third is appreciation – treating others as precious and valuable. Everyone is happy to feel valued and respected so to instil a sense of worth in people, whether it is a wife, husband, child, employee, employer, church member, prison inmate, traffic warden or official – people from all walks of like – is like waving a magic wand at them.

Recognising and respecting others, great or small, is part of our divine heritage. (Leviticus 19:18; John 13:34) When we respond to others with appropriate respect, kindness and care, we are doing what God requires of us. We also attract them to us. We are all made in God's image and we are all valuable and need one another. Caring for one another is a wise and virtuous act. Remember always that love delights in praise.

- Smile

Cheer up, Rach! For a couple about to be married Rach and Max didn't look too excited when they were photographed while out shopping on the eve of the lavish wedding ceremony. The smiles finally broke out shortly before the wedding, as Max arrived at the plush hotel. Orchids and hundreds of white roses were delivered and the ballroom was adorned with swathes of silk. Rach said, 'I'm going all out with a meringue dress. I'm so excited.' 'Let's hope the smiles break out better on the big day than they did on the shopping trip', a tabloid cruelly commented.

A sincere smile says a lot and works miracles to attract people. A smile speaks of love and friendliness, causing the other person to smile back because the very act of smiling helps people feel connected to one another. Smiling cheers you up and, without exception, easy-to-know people are always smiling. A smile is a magic switch that turns on a friendly feeling, whether paying someone a compliment, accepting a favour, asking a favour and is even effective when using 'plain talk', or when you meet someone for the first time. A smile is an important human asset of which you should always make use. Pay someone a compliment with a smile and watch how it multiplies the compliment. Ask someone a favour with a smile and watch how he will be compelled to grant it. Accept a favour from someone else with a smile and watch the joy in his face.

The biggest myth about smiling is that we smile when we're happy. In fact, it's the other way around. Smiling and laughter make us happier. At times, of course, you don't feel like smiling, but feeling is only the process of thought. Happiness is not a matter of 'feeling' but a deep-seated sense of contentment born from the fulfilment of one's responsibility as a human being. It relates to the state of the whole person. As the Greek philosopher, Aristotle, commented, contentment is an enduring sense of well-being that may even persist when a person is experiencing pain. Our well-being and contentment is in Christ Jesus. 'He has given us all things that pertain to life.' (2 Peter 1:3) and 'We are to rejoice always.' (Philippians 4:4) Remember always that laugh, and the world laughs with you. Weep and you weep alone.

- White magic

The art of listening, sometimes referred to as 'white magic', is a secret that has helped many gain victories in life. Making the necessary changes and transformations in life is impossible without listening to good counsel. Before we can do anything new and reasonable, it is imperative to listen to those who are wiser and more experienced than ourselves. Paul Godawa says that without the art of listening, life's journey is like trying to reach an unknown destination without paying any attention to the traffic signals and signposts. The signposts leading to victory are God, who created you, and the people who walk in front of you, which include teachers, mentors, pastors, parents and friends.

Jesus often pointed out the importance of listening to his disciples, (Mark 4:9; Matthew 11:15) and there are about eight different scriptures concerned with listening in the Book of Revelation, because the fruits of listening are wisdom, stature, maturity and favour. These were the things Jesus desired from infancy. He started to listen to wise men and teachers of the law at the aged of 12, (Luke 2:46) and Jesus called it at first 'being occupied by my Father's business'. (Luke 2:48) We hear with our ears, but a deeper kind of listening is with the mind and heart. Listening becomes helpful for honest seekers. Remember always that he that will not be counselled cannot be helped.

- Who to listen to

We live in a society flooded with huge waves of information. There is someone talking to us almost all the time, on the radio and television, in the media, our friends, parents, wife or husband. There are many voices trying to get our attention with the power to shape our hearts and minds. Listening to the right people and paying attention to what is important is the key to a good character that lasts for a lifetime, even for eternity.

To accomplish your purpose in life you need access to information. Information is power. The nature of what we listen to shows where we are going and influences the way we feel, how we see the future and how we see ourselves. Be careful whom you listen to, for he who influences our ears influences our desires, and he who controls our desires controls our lives. Surround yourself with creative people, those who are full of ideas, zeal and faith and who want to do something with their lives and transform your life forever. The measure of our happiness depends on the advice we take. Stay well away from fools, 'For you will not find knowledge on his lips.' (Proverbs 14:7) Remember, 'He who walks with the wise shall be wise.'

Not everyone with life experience will be willing to share their knowledge. Our hunger and determination will, however, lead us to the right people. At times we must leave our 'comfort zone' but when a student is ready, a teacher comes. Remember always that good counsel has no price. Every word of God is pure; He is a shield.

- A bossy and dominant attitude never draws people

Getting along with other people brings enormous personal satisfaction; the ability of not trampling on other people's egos is a great leveller in the workplace. In the contemporary workplace, bossy and dominant people seldom get promotion. Lording over people is unacceptable; arrogance is outmoded and people that bully and put others down often find themselves left by the wayside, professionally anyway. These days, generally speaking, the workplace ethos seems to be that if you show people they are important, precious and valuable you get more out of them; productivity improves, absenteeism drops, and the wheels of social interaction turn more easily.

Peace and harmony, whether in the workplace, family or elsewhere, do not come about by chance but are accomplished through deliberate effort. Make the choice to live life according to the principles of wisdom and openness, make your behaviour consistent and persist in living a noble life governed by love.

- Taming a lion into a lamb

James Edward Oglethorpe (1696–1789) founded British Georgia in America. He envisaged it as a place where the poor and destitute could start afresh and where persecuted Protestant sects could find refuge. He sought permission from the King of England to found the colony in the New World, persuading the king for many weeks with all sorts of 'logical arguments' until, finally, the king became interested when Oglethorpe suggested naming the colony after him.

It is said that a hungry dog is a mean dog, as well-fed dogs seldom fight. We are all the more agreeable, understanding and cooperative if the ego – that God-given, innate sense of personal worth – is nourished with genuine compliments and real praise. By identifying little things in others that we can compliment, we enhance their ego, thus helping them love themselves more and turning the lion within them into a lamb.

Difficult people are often screwed up inside and do not necessarily share in your intentions and ideals. Sometimes the hungry ego manifests in downright malicious and thoughtless behaviour where the individual appears to be oblivious to the effect their behaviour has on others, and appears to be determined to continue to do what suits them. These individuals can be angry, bad-tempered, unpleasant, despicable and obnoxious, and have a total lack of respect for others, are malicious and abusive, intent on deliberately causing others harm.

Save yourself a lot of time and do not be drawn into arguments with people like this if they aim some unhelpful remark at you. The worst thing is to become aggressive and respond angrily to them: do not reflect back their dark behaviour. Instead, relax, let go of the unpleasantness, pull back your emotions and energies; release feelings of anger, frustration and blame and just get on with the important aspects of your life, '... make every effort to do what leads to peace.' (Romans 14:19) Remember always that the secret wall of a town is peace.

- Troublemakers

An England footballer was arrested over claims that he had drunkenly attacked and racially abused a nightclub doorman and then urinated in the street. 'What kind of behaviour is that for a premiership footballer? We are all absolutely disgusted by his behaviour', the doorman commented.

No one wants to be labelled a troublemaker, but that is precisely what many of us demonstrate by our deeds. Many people claim to be wise but act foolishly. True wisdom is measured by the depth of our character just as we identify a tree by the type of fruit it produces.

Foolishness allows our deeds to create disorder while wisdom creates peace and goodness. Avoid escalating conflicts or fanning the fire of discord. Avoid sowing the seeds of contention, rumours and lies. The wise do not let gossip hurt others or jeopardise friendships. They do not speak aggressively in response to vitriol from another but answer gently to harsh words. The wise do not mock, look down upon or ignore the poor man, and they choose to forgive and disregard the wrong people have done them. God loves the peacemakers. (Matthew 5:9) Remember always that peace makes plenty. Forgive anyone you are holding a grudge against, so that your father in heaven will forgive your sins too'. (Mark 11:25)

- Trust

Building trust between people can take a considerable amount of time. If individuals experience a breach of trust or break other's trust in them, it can be destroyed very quickly and may never be restored to its former level. Breaking trust can occur in more subtle ways: making a joke at another's expense; being judgemental about another's behaviour, attitudes or beliefs or communicating rejection or non acceptance, either verbally or non-verbally. On the other side of the coin, trust is developed in seven ways:

- OPENNESS: sharing information, ideas, thoughts, reactions and when appropriate, feelings
- SHARING: offering resources to other people to help them achieve their goals
- TRUSTWORTHINESS: if other people are justified in placing their trust in

you, they experience beneficial and not harmful consequences

- ACCEPTANCE: holding other people's points of view and values in high regard
- SUPPORT: recognising other people's strengths and allowing them to function without your intervention
- COOPERATION: working together to achieve a mutual goal
- RECIPROCATION: appropriate reciprocation when a person shares their thoughts or feelings with you.

As a member of a family, it is essential that you develop trust with one another and they have trust in you in order for you to relate to one another effectively.

15

TRANSCENDENCE

Is God real?
In United Kingdom, figures for 'I believe in God' are always between 74 per cent and 77 per cent every year. A recent opinion poll also asked 'Do you definitely not believe in God?' and only 4 per cent said 'Yes'. Most people have a wavering belief, or don't know. 'Is God real?' is one of the most and hard to understand questions we can ask. Many people have therefore given up trying to find the answer. Admittedly, it is tough to believe in someone we have never seen.

The simple statement that God created the heavens and the earth (Genesis 1:1) is one of the most challenging concepts confronting the modern mind. The vast galaxy we live in is spinning at the incredible speed of 400,000 mile an hour. But even at this breakneck speed, our galaxy still needs 200 million years to make one rotation. And there are over one billion other galaxies just like ours in the universe. Some scientists say that the number of stars in creation is equal to all the grains of all the sands on all the beaches of the world. Yet this complex sea of spinning stars functions with remarkable order and efficiency. To say that the universe 'just happened' or 'evolved' requires more faith than to believe that God is behind these amazing statistics. God truly did create a wonderful universe.

Think about a car. Though we have never met the manufacturer, or have any idea about how cars are made, the car is indeed real as it was made by someone. Let us therefore build our life on the power and love of God. In the hours of trial we should look beyond the mountains to the Lord who made them. He is the source of our help. (Psalm 121:2, 5)

God is still unknown!
Many years ago, a man by the name of Paul travelled to Athens. He found that the Athenians had built an idol to the unknown God for the fear of missing blessings or receiving punishment. He realised that though they were very religious, they did not know the true God (Acts 17:22-33). Today we have a 'Christian society' (between 74 per cent and 77 per cent who believe in God), but God is still unknown.

From ancient times, man has been longing for transcendence. People have always felt the need to worship a god and no race has been known which has not had a god of some kind. All the great religions of the world teach that there is one God who controls the universe. Brahmins, Hindus, Buddhists, Muslims, and Confucians all seek a God whom they can know and love. In many civilisations of ancient times, people believed in one or several gods. All of these religions prove that God is real.

The mystery

Many a time when we refer to God, there is an element of controversy and doubt. Think about this. 'No man has been able to explain the mysteries of the universe or the mysteries of life. We are surrounded by mysteries. The operation of the body is a profound mystery, so is electricity in our homes. The fact that we do not understand totally the mysteries of our bodies or electricity or a gas engine does not keep us from using or enjoying them' writes Dale Carnegie. The fact that we do not understand the mysteries of God, no longer keeps us from enjoying the richer and happier life that Christianity brings.

Who is God?

His name

Most people have at least two names – a first name, which their parents choose for them; and a surname, or family name. A surname shows what family a person belongs to and is usually the same as their father's. God has a personal name and his name and various titles tell us his identity and character. He is called YAHWEH. YAHWEH is derived from the Hebrew word for 'I AM'. The name eventually ceased to be pronounced because later Jews thought it too holy to be uttered and feared violating the second commandment. 'You shall not misuse the name of the Lord your God, for the Lord will not hold anyone guiltless who misuses his name ...' (Exodus 20:7)

Yahweh means 'I AM' or 'I WILL BE'. New World Translation reads, 'I shall prove to be what I shall prove to be'. He will prove to be or cause himself to become whatever is needed in order to fulfill his promises. J.B Rotherham's translation reads 'I will become whatever I please'. Whatever the situation or need, God will become the solution to that need. No matter what obstacle looms before us, no matter how difficult the predicament in which we find ourselves, he would become whatever is needed in order to deliver us from bondage and bring us victory. As parents become versatile – teachers, nurses, judges, providers etc – there is nothing God would not become in order to care for us in the best possible way.

God called himself I AM, a name describing his power and character as the dependable and faithful God who desires the full trust of his people and who can fulfill whatever he promises. In a world where values, morals and laws change constantly, we can find stability and security in our unchanging God.

His nature

If you want someone to get to know you, you might tell the person your name. God's name is full of meaning. He has used human understanding of the significance of names and applied it to himself in order to reveal his nature to mankind.

El Shaddai (Genesis 17:1): The Almighty, all-powerful one, constantly pouring out nourishment to his children and meeting their needs

Yahweh (Lord or Jehovah) (Exodus 3:15; Psalm 83: 18; Isaiah 26:4): The one who always is, the constant I AM, the existing one

Jehovah Shammah (Ezekiel 48:35): The Lord is there, He is constantly present with us

Jehovah Shalom (Judges 6:24): The Lord our peace and wholeness

Jehovah Jireh (Genesis 22:14):The Lord will provide for us

Jehovah Nissi (Exodus 17:15): The Lord our banner and our victory

Jehovah Tsidkenu (Jeremiah 23:6; Jeremiah 33:16): The Lord who clothes us with his righteousness, the Lord our righteousness

Jehovah Rapha (Exodus 15:26): The Lord that heals us

Jehovah Ra ah (Psalm 23:1): The Lord who is our loving guiding shepherd.

Jehovah Mekadish-Kem (Exodus 31:13): The Lord who sanctifies us

Jehovah Yasha-Gaal (Isaiah 49:26; Isaiah 60:16): The Lord our Saviour and Redeemer

El Elyon (Genesis 14:18; 2 Samuel 22:14): The Most High God, the ruler and possessor of heaven and earth; the one who is in charge

All the storms that threaten to be over our heads are beneath the feet of God (1 Corinthians 15:25-28).

All things are possible

God is unique in power. His name is 'I AM'. He can cause himself to become whatever he chooses because he has an unlimited power. He has the ability to act, to carry out his will. Great is his strength and speed. God is vigorous in power and possesses an abundance of dynamic energy; the ever-plentiful, inexhaustible source of power that does not depend upon outside source for energy. He uses this power to create, destroy, protect, restore, reveal important aspects of his personality and standards, fulfill his will, to benefit us and use it on behalf of those who love him – to do whatever suits his purpose (Isaiah 40:10–18). 'I know that you can do all things. No plan of yours can be thwarted, writes Job. (Job 42:2)

God's power should no way shy us away from approaching him. We should come to him for protection. God's power reassures us that nothing can prevent him from helping and strengthening those whom he loves. (Psalm 118:6) God's power is so immense and his means of exerting it is so effective that nothing can stand in his way. Without doubt, with him all things are possible. (Matthew 19:26) Is anything too hard for the Lord? (Genesis 18:14) Of course not! This is what I always do. I have developed a habit of inserting my specific needs into the question, 'Is this day in my life too hard for the Lord? Is this habit I'm trying to break too hard for him? Is this communication problem I'm having too hard for him?' Asking the question this way reminds me that God is personally involved in my life and nudges me to ask for his power to help me.

Creative powers

God's creativity is inexhaustible and this, of course separates him from everything he has created and thereby gives him the intrinsic right to wield exclusive sovereign power over all the universe. God has not stopped working altogether. He still works to bring his purpose to fulfilment. (Isaiah 46:11-13) When he comes to our lives, his beauty will be seen. He will make our lives beautiful. When you feel worthless or even begin to hate yourself, remember that God's creative power is still at work and his spirit is ready and willing to work within you. Besides, knowing that we are the only thing made in God's image and thus share many of his characteristics – reason, creativity, speech, self-determination – and have been given a remarkable privilege to rule over the earth provides a solid basis of creativity.

The creation story teaches us how God gave form to the 'formless and empty' universe. In the same way, if we are dissatisfied with the way things are as we look around, we must not be content with the status quo. After all, why shouldn't we have a better lifestyle, a better self-image, a better community... and a better world? And why shouldn't you and everybody else enjoy a better future full of hope. We can change our world. We are incredibly creative, that image of God is in us. (Genesis 1:26) We see the unacceptable: do we not care? We see what it is: do we see what it could be? Things could be different. Stretch yourself further and develop the necessary skills to accomplish your dream.

Jesus tells the parable of the king's ten servants who were given money to put to work. The King punished the man who did nothing to use the money. (Luke 19:20-27) Like the King in the story, God has given you gifts to use for the benefit of the world. One day in the future you might be asked if you were part of the dramatic, positive changes of your world.

God of justice
God is the supreme judge but justice from his point of view, is more than the fair application of the rules of law. What marks the justice of God is just and mercy. He is gracious and righteous and full of compassion. (Psalm 116:5) By means of this, He can express tender mercy towards a repentant sinner while maintaining His standards of perfect justice. (Romans 3:21-23)

God's justice moves Him to show faithfulness and loyalty towards us. He never for one moment abandons those who are loyal to Him. Furthermore, His justice makes Him sensitive to the needs of the afflicted. He makes sure victims of life are cared for and He always becomes their judge and protector. 'He defends the cause of the fatherless and the widow, and loves the aliens'. (Deuteronomy 10:18) 'A father of the fatherless, and a judge of the widows is God in his holy habitation'. (Psalm 68:5)

He is not swayed by material wealth or outward appearance. He cares for people from all walks of life. (Acts 10:34; Deuteronomy 10:17) God's justice also means He will not forever tolerate a situation that brings reproach upon His name. He will not shield willful sinners from the adverse judgement that their cause deserves. (Exodus 34:6-7) Although our sins deserve severe judgement, God has chosen to show love and mercy to all who seek him.

God of wisdom

God possesses wisdom in the absolute sense. He is the source of all true wisdom. (Proverbs 2:6) Contemplate God's wisdom and you will be lost for words. He sees far into the distance of time – future. (Job 39:29) The Bible contains hundreds of prophecies or history written in advance. The outcome of wars, and the rise and fall of world powers were foretold in advance. God's wisdom is apparent in every bit of creation around us. Take a look at people, seeing each one as God's unique creation, each with his own special talents, abilities and gifts. As we observe our natural surroundings, we have to appreciate God for his creativity.

God is willing to give us this wisdom (James 1:5) to those who ask Him. Think about this, 'Jesus, the greatest man who ever lived on our earth and the son of God, though the wisest of the sons of men did not rely on his own wisdom but spoke as his father directed him.' It is imperative for us to seek wisdom from God to enable us to face trials with 'pure joy' and have practical insight with spiritual implication

God of love

The superficiality of our world makes everything including love shallow and empty. 'I love you' a young man tells his girl friend only to get what he wants. A parent who believes in his family still continue to indulge in illicit affairs. As the lazy ones are supposed to learn responsibility from the proverbial ant ,(Proverbs 6:6) we who have confused love with lust, must plug in to God's kind of love which is always directed outwards towards others not inward towards ourselves.

God sees worth in us. (Matthew 10:29-31) He values us so much that he remembers our every detail – genetic code, years of memories and experiences. He delights in our good qualities and in the efforts we put forth. (Hebrews 10:6) He even has a book of remembrance for us. (Malachi 3:16) He looks beyond our imperfections and sees potential. No matter our circumstances, he does what is necessary to restore us to perfection/ (Acts 3:21; Romans 8:20-22) He sees the good in us in which we may not see or simply overlook, and develops it. He has made provision for our salvation and peace by giving gifts to people to preach the gospel of hope, the Holy Spirit to reveal the truth and the privilege of prayer to ask him anything we desire. Our distress is distressing to him. (Psalm 63:9; 1 Peter 5:7; Matthew 11:28) 'He that is touching you is touching my eyeball.' (Zechariah 2:8) He feels for us. Where we hurt, he hurts.

The good God

There is no poverty where there is virtue, no riches where virtue is not; Good heart conquers ill fortune; a house is a fine house when good folks are within. Goodness primarily refers to virtue and moral excellence. It takes the initiative, actively seeking ways to benefit others. This is God who is unique in His goodness. He is good to all. He has compassion on all he has made. (Psalm 145:9)

Everyone who has lived has benefited from His goodness. He gives rains from heaven and fruitful seasons, filling hearts to the full with food and good cheer. (Acts 14:17) He makes His sun rise upon wicked and good people. (Matthew 5:45) He is the source of all that is truly good. He is the giver of every good gift and every perfect present. (James 1:17) In his infinite goodness, He has given us a body that is 'wonderfully made with senses designed to help us perceive his works and delight in them. (Psalm 139:14)

God's spiritual provisions can do us even more good than the physical kind can do, for they lead to everlasting life. (Matthew 4:4) He is merciful and gracious, slow to anger and abundant in loving kindness and truth. (Exodus 35:19; Exodus 34:6) He is not cold and tyrannical, rather gentle and kind towards us. He does not lie to us. (Numbers 23:19; Titus 1:2) His promises are completely reliable. He is far too good to lie and dispenses an abundance of truth. He is not close-guarded or secretive rather He generously releases His unlimited wisdom to us. (James 1:5) His motives are full of goodness. We must trust Him completely for He wants nothing but good for those who love Him.

The most loyal God

A few years ago, writes Pat Mesiti, a lady came to his office with a desire to work with young people. She decided to come on staff without pay. She was not skilled but was willing to learn. One day a man said to her, 'You better enjoy this while it lasts, because one day the organisation won't exist.' You should have seen the look on the lady's face. She said, 'There is no reason on God's earth why the dream has to end. The only ones who could kill it are us.' Today she basically runs the functions of the organization.

Loyalty is kindness that lovingly attaches itself to an object and does not let go until its purpose in connection with that object is realised. It's rooted in love. It's warm and its very manifestation indicates that a relationship exists between the person who displays the quality and the one towards whom it is shown. It is not fickle and unlike waves of the sea which can be blown about by changing winds. It has the stability and strength to overcome the most daunting of obstacles.

Although loyal ones are rare, we can rely on God's loving kindness and loyalty which never fails. God is very loyal (Revelation 15:4) in all His works (Psalm 145:17) and remains true to His standards. He is always loyal to His promises. Not a promise failed out of all the good promises Hhe has made to us (Isaiah 55:11). We can be confident that, God will never dissappoint us. (Isaiah 49:23; Romans 5:5) His loving kindness is to time indefinite. (Psalm 136:1) He always come to our aid when we are in distress and guards our souls out of the hand of the wicked ones. (Psalm 97:10)

The Ancient of Days

God has existed for an eternity before anyone or anything else on the universe came into being. From time indefinite to time indefinite He is God (Psalm 90:2). He never began. He has always been. In truth it is difficult for our limited minds to comprehend the existence of God, as the minds of little children hardly understand the realities of life or as the operation of ultrasonic is a profound mystery to the ordinary mind. We are physical beings and thereby put too much stock in what we can see with our eyes. God is a spiritual being, invisible to human eyes. (John 4:24) Nevertheless as we readily accept the reality of wind, radio waves, electric currents and ultrasonic, though invisible to the naked eyes, God is far more real.

We are free to follow and enjoy God rather than spend our time trying to figure Him out. He is the same yesterday and today and forever. (Hebrews 13:8) He is the Ancient of Days' who makes known the end from the beginning, from ancient times what is still to come (Isaiah 46:10). He is unique in his knowledge, experience and in his control of the future. When we are tempted to pursue anything that promises pleasure, comfort, peace and security apart from God, we must remember 'Have God and have all'.

The holy God

Think about this, 'Nick is very brilliant and intelligent. He desires to be a member of the local Church of God. His own errors in life have passed over his head. He has grown numb and carried the crushing burden of guilty conscience. His self-condemned heart insisted that he can never come close to God. God is holy so people who come to him should be holy. He has a sense of exaggerated awareness of holiness which put him off from responding to God'. Nick's circumstance is not different from many people especially people who struggle with a negative view of themselves to draw closer to God.

Holiness does not mean self-righteousness or piety. It means 'separation'. It is applied to that which is separated from common use or held sacred. It conveys the idea of cleanliness and purity. The holiness of God simply means He is separate from all creation in that he alone is the most high. He is separated from all sinfulness and therefore can never be tainted by the slightest trace of sin or evil. He can never turn corrupt, dissolute or abusive. Everything at him is clean, pure and upright.

God's holiness does not imply coldness, remoteness, cruelty and wanting to repel people. He is willing to view us as holy no matter how imperfect and sinful we are. Listen to him, 'Come now, let us reason together, says the lord. Though your sins are like scarlet they shall be as white as snow, though they are as red as crimson, they shall be like wool. If you are willing and obedient, you will eat the good of the land.' (Isaiah 1:18-19) He is the source of all holiness and is ready to impart it generously to us. God loves what is upright and pure. He hates sin. But He does not hate sinners. As long as we view sin as He does – hating what is bad, loving what is good and strive to follow in Christ footsteps, God forgives our sins.

God has told us enough about Himself in the Bible – for us to be saved by faith and to serve him. We must not use the limitation of our knowledge about creation as an excuse to reject God's claim on our life. If we are ready to return to God, He will be ready to receive us. The tragedy of life is that some people will not turn to God until their world has crashed in around them. Then the sorrow and pain seem to open their eyes to what God has been saying all along. Avoid 'Had I known'.

16

DOES GOD CARE?

The news these days is hardly comforting. Current events are so grim that we often can't decide whether or not we dare watch the six o'clock news. The world is awash with wars, acts of terror, suffering, crime, disunity and mistrust – evils that may soon affect us directly if they have not done so already. Nearly 400 people were killed in an all night assault in Sri Lanka's war zone forcing thousands to flee for makeshift shelters. Probably many more than the 378 reported were killed in the violence but they were buried where they fell, wrote a tabloid in May 2009. If God is all-powerful, loving, wise and just why is His world, the world He created, in a total mess? If God exists or cares, the world would be a better place to live.

If He cares about us and our problems, would He not prevent such things from happening?

Why does God allow sufferings?

Far be it from God to do evil, from the Almighty to do wrong. (Job 34:10) God doesn't sin and is never unjust. We may have elements of truth in our speeches, unfortunately the nuggets of truth are buried under layers of false assumptions and conclusions. The truth is that our world which reflects an invisible spirit world, is lying in the power and influence of the wicked one, Satan. (1 John 5:19) Satan is hateful, deceptive and is misleading the entire inhabited world (Revelation 12:9) into hatred, deceit and cruelty.

We are also responsible for the misery. Our greediness, selfishness and ignorance (imperfection and sinfulness) lead us to struggle for dominance, resulting in wars, oppression and sufferings. (Ecclesiastes 4:1; Ecclesiastes 8:9) Moreover, some people may suffer because they happen to be in the wrong place at the wrong time (Ecclesiastes 9:11). The world is unfair. The world is finite and sin has twisted life, making it what God did not intend. He cares for us. (1 Peter 5:7) He hates wickedness and the suffering it causes. (Isaiah 55:8-9) He has a plan and will judge evildoers in his time. Don't let the iniquities of life keep you from God. God is in the position to do you most good. (Isaiah 40:28-29)

False conclusion

In frustration we jump to the false conclusion that God does not care. Wrong assumptions always lead to wrong conclusions. It is tempting to take our limited experiences and jump to conclusions about life. We hardly have all the facts. Think about this, 'Many people endure great pain, but ultimately they find that some greater good comes from it'. When you are struggling, don't assume the worst. I have also observed that in frustration, many people wallow in self-pity. Our affliction lures us towards feeling sorry for ourselves. We may feel like blaming God always forgetting that life's trials, whether allowed by God or sent by God, can be the means for development and refinement.

Moreover, when we are suffering, we often feel as though our pain will never end. In comparison to eternity, our suffering would last only 'a little while'. Invariably some people would be strengthened and delivered in their lifetimes. Others would be released from their pains through death. The truth, however, is that all things work together for good in them that love God (Romans 8:28) and we are assured of an eternal life with Christ where there will be no suffering. (Revelation 21:1) I wish we asked ourselves when facing trials, 'What can I learn and how can I grow?' rather than 'Who did this to me and how can I get out of it?' Learn how to carry your worries, stresses and daily struggles to God. (1 Peter 5:7)

God's plan for us

Thousands of residents have returned to their homes after being driven out by the threat of wildfires. 'The blaze which has consumed 3,400 hectares since Tuesday has destroyed 31 homes' (Met ro, 11May 2009). How does God feel about what is going on in the world and in our lives. Is this what God purposed for us and the rest of the world? No. He feels hurt at his heart when badness fills the world. He hates to see the suffering that is taking place worldwide. He hates to see people suffer. He has a plan for the future. The plans are good and full of hope. He is unique in his knowledge and in his control of the future. His consistent purpose is to carry out what he has planned.

God will definitely bring changes on earth. He will wipe every tear from our eyes. There will be no more deaths or mourning or crying or pain, for the old order of things has passed away. (Revelation 21:4) Then will the lame leap like a deer and the mute tongue shout for joy. Water will gush forth in the wilderness and streams in the desert. (Isaiah 35:6) Then the eyes of the blind will be opened, and the ears of the deaf unstopped. (Isaiah 35:5) All who are in their graves will hear hHis voice and come out. (John 5:28-29) No one will say I am ill and the sins of those that dwell there will be forgiven. (Isaiah 33:24) There will come to be plenty of grain on the land. (Psalm 72:16)

Our new home with God will defy description. We will not be disappointed by it in any way. All people everywhere are invited to be a citizen of the new world. God is giving it freely. This is our future. This is our hope. This is our destiny and inheritance. God cares. God is good.

God's loving purpose

Our heavenly father has good plans for us. God's plan for us is always for good. Unknown plans can be frightening, but when the plans belong to God, we can be rest assured that we can expect something marvellous. He cares about what we do and the details of our lives. Our heavenly father's loving purpose for us include the following, writes Bob Gordon:

He is always willing to answer prayer (Isaiah 65:24; Matthew 7:1)

He longs for men to be His children (Jeremiah 3:19)

He delights to show mercy (Micah 7:18)

He purposes that we may have life and have it to the full (John 10:10)

He wants to set us free from fear (John 14:1; Psalm 118:5-9)

He desires to give man an eternal home (John 14:2-3)

He wants all mankind to be saved (1 Timothy 2:3-4)

He wants to take care of our needs (1 Peter 5:7)

God cares. We can be certain that the one who gave us spiritual birth will never abandon us or fail us. Before we call he will answer, while we are still speaking he will hear. (Isaiah 65:24)

God who fights for his people

Like Napoleon Bonaparte, Alexander the Great and other military commanders, God commands a vast army of angelic forces. He fights to remove wickedness; to protect his name and to defend his people. Starting with Moses, Joshua and continuing on through to the period of the Judges and the Kings of Israel, God fought for his people, giving them victories over their enemies. He has not changed and still intervenes on our behalf. He desires to protect His people. He goes before us and fights. He gives us many dramatic victories over our circumstances.

Think about this, 'The Lord will fight for you, you need only to be still'. (Exodus 14:14) The Israelites were hostile and despairing, but Moses encouraged them to watch the wonderful way through which God would rescue them. Moses had a positive attitude. When it looked as if they were trapped, Moses called upon God to intervene. Unlike the Israelites, we may not be chased by an army, but we may still feel trapped by circumstances. Instead of giving in to despair, we should adopt Moses' attitude to 'call upon God', 'stand firm' and see the 'deliverance' God will bring.

God our refuge

Because of its size and splendid soaring flight, the eagle has always been regarded as the king of birds. The Roman soldiers used to carry the figure of an eagle on a pole when they marched into battle. Eagles have also been used as national emblems, or signs, by various European countries, and the bald-headed eagle is the emblem of the United States. The eagle uses its broad, strong wings to fly and protect its tender nestlings from the scorching sun and the cold wind. God is capable of protecting us just as the eagle safeguards its young ones. Think about this: 'God is our refuge and strength, an ever-present help in troubled times. Therefore we will not fear, though the earth gives way and the mountains fall into the heart of the sea'. (Psalm 46:1-3)

God is our refuge even in the face of total destruction. He is our eternal refuge and can provide strength in any circumstances. He is our shepherd. (Psalm 23:1; Psalm 100:3) As the effectiveness of the shepherd depends on the complete dependence of the sheep on him for provision, guidance and protection, we must not be mere passive people but obedient followers, wise enough to follow one who will lead us in the right places and in right ways.

The promise of divine protection does not mean that God is guaranteeing us a problem-free life. Time and unforeseen occurrences befall us all. (Ecclesiastes 9:11) We may face severe adversities, poverty, war, sickness and death. God, however, knows how to deliver us out of troubles.

The secret service

The Secret Service of United States' principal duty is the protection of the president of the United States and members of his family, the vice president and family, cabinet officers and senior diplomatic officers of the United Nations and foreign governments. The Secret Service was charged with protection of the president in 1901, just after the assassination of President William McKinley. Secret Service agents in plain clothes are close to the president at all times, wherever he goes. It operates one of the largest and most efficient burglar alarm systems in the world. Like the Secret Service agents, God guards his people and is always close to us at all times, wherever we go.

God always identifies with the pains of his people. He does not just feel for us, he moves to act on our behalf. He is more than 'just sympathetic awareness' of our troubles. He responds to them. He is not deaf to our cries. His tender compassion moves him to relieve our suffering and to take strong, decisive action. He knows that, in times of trouble, we need him more than ever, and he is always near. (Psalm 34:15, 18) 'Can a woman forget her nursing child that she should not have compassion on the child she has borne? Yes, they may forget, yet I will not forget you. See, I have engraved you on the palms of my hands, your walls are ever before me'. (Isaiah 49:15-16; James 5:11) It is difficult to imagine that a mother would forget to nourish and care for her nursing and helpless child. Never should we doubt that God will fulfil His promises. He will even do the impossible to make them come through.

God who lifts burden

Capital punishment is the death penalty for a crime. It is usually carried out by hanging, electrocution, beheading, injection or firing squad. Because of the work of social reformers the death penalty is now much less common. God is more than these reformers who fought against capital punishment. God is aware of our limitations – mere dust, (Psalm 103:14) having frailties and weaknesses. He understands how powerful sin is – a potent force that has man in its deadly grip. (Romans 3:9; Romans 5:21)

No matter how earnestly we may yearn, we can never overcome sin by our own effort. We must approach God for support. He has given us Jesus, His greatest gift as a ransom, so that we might have forgiveness of sin. It is only through the blood of Jesus that we are cleansed from our sins. We are justified by Christ's blood. God pardons or take away our guilt, iniquity and transgressions of those who seek His forgiveness. When He forgives our errors and iniquities He remembers no more. (Jeremiah 31:34) He would not bring our sins again and again in order to accuse or punish us over and over. He forgives and forgets.

The feeling of remorse is healthy because sin passes over our head a heavy load and crushing burden of a pained conscience, (Psalm 38:4, 8) It is imperative to take positive steps to correct our mistakes. In spite of the mistakes we may have made we should never conclude that we are beyond the reach of God's mercy. God does not hate the sinner if he truly repents and regrets his sinful course. God hates sin and desires that we come to Him for forgiveness of sin. (1 John 1:9; Isaiah 1:18, 19)

You may be going through troubles. The truth is that God has already done a lot for you, and He longs to do more. The evidence of this care may come through the people that come into your life to meet your needs and encourage you. It may come through a deep peace in your heart as you express your trust in God and cast all your cares on Him. It may come through the supply of your physical needs or grace and strength to endure great difficulty. (2 Corinthians 12:9; Philippians 4:11)

Cast all your worries on Him because He cares. Prayer is your life-line. A diver cannot live without the life-line through which air comes. Prayer is to the soul as breathing is to the human body. It is our direct line with the 'spiritual head office'. When the walkie-talkie set is switched on, every word is heard by head office which keeps a constant listening watch. Prayer links you directly with your leader and God. Advice, help and guidance are constantly available to you. God will make a way where there seems to be no way.

17

God's greatest gifts

Around 1100, Saint Nicholas became a popular symbol of gift giving in many European countries. According to legend, he brought presents to children on the eve of his feast day, 6 December. Nonreligious figures replaced Saint Nicholas in certain countries soon after the Reformation and December 25 became the day for giving gifts. Today Santa Claus brings presents to children in many countries. Some countries have their version such as Father Christmas in Britain, Pere Noel in France and Weihnachsmann in Germany.

God, by His divine power has given us everything we need for life and godliness. (2 Peter 1:3) Of all the things we receive, spiritual gifts bring us the most happiness and lasting good. Six most precious gifts of God we must gratefully receive are Jesus Christ, Prayer, the Bible, the Holy Spirit, the Ministers and eternal life.

God loved the world so much that he gave His only Son, Jesus Christ, that whoever believes in Him shall not perish but have eternal life (John 3:16). Nothing could surprise Jesus as a gift. God has also provided us with the Bible, His word. The Bible is not a collection of stories, fables, myths or merely human ideas about God. It is God's message about His person, plan and purposes for our lives. (2 Peter 1:20) It's a manual of life. In addition to the Bible and Jesus Christ it is the gift of the Holy Spirit. The Holy Spirit is the believer's helper. He is our comforter, counsellor, advocate, intercessor and guide. The single greatest key to eternal success in any Christian endeavour is allowing the full work of the Holy Spirit in and through us. Jesus said that He would build His church (Matthew 16:18) and He has chosen to do this by giving gifts of men as leaders to the church, who will prepare God's people for works of service. (Ephesians 4: 11-13) Nor is that all. God has made available the gift of eternal life (Romans 6:23), a new life with God that begins on earth and continues for ever with God. Since they are gifts, they must be gratefully received. God will not force them on us but rather to those who sincerely desire them.

Michael Marnu

Jesus Christ

We often introduce ourselves by name and call people by name. Someone who uses your name makes you feel warm. Calling someone by name calls on something very deep in them. The Scriptures use many names to describe Jesus. Jesus expresses His work on earth – 'to save and to deliver'. This is affirmed by the explanation the angel gave Joseph after telling him to name the virgin-born child Jesus: 'For He Will save His People from their Sins'. (Matthew 1:21) Christ literally means 'the Anointed One'. In the Old Testament, forms of its Hebrew equivalent 'Messiah' were applied to prophets, (1 King 19:16) priests (Lev 4:5,16) and kings, (1 Samuel 24:6,10) in the sense that all of them were anointed with oil, the symbolism that God had set them aside for their respective offices. But the pre-eminent Anointed One would be the promised Messiah, for He would be anointed by God's spirit to be the ultimate Prophet, Priest and King (Isaiah 61:1; John 3:34). Saviour means ' one who provides salvation. The word also means deliverer, protector or preserver. In ancient Greek society, the term was applied not only to gods but also to human beings whose significant actions brought some type of benefit to others. In Luke 2:11, the angel announces to the shepherds the birth of a ' Saviour, who is Christ the Lord', 'one who will offer Himself as a sacrifice to provide redemption for all.' The scripture's emphasis on Jesus as Saviour can be seen in the summary of Jesus' mission in Luke 19:10 'to seek and to save that which was lost'. Emmanuel means God with us, because Jesus was the Son of God and He lived among us (Matthew 1:23). He is the only child who can truly be called Wonderful, Counsellor, and the Prince of Peace. (Isaiah 9:6).

Jesus' key to life was love. He taught humanity to show love for his neighbour. Love was His golden rule. He emptied himself of His glory and humbled Himself to serve. He became little, weak and vulnerable and gave His life as a ransom price for the release of others. So He allowed himself to become a victim of gross injustice in the courts, and as they crucified Him He prayed for His enemies. Then in the awful God-forsaken darkness He bore our sins in His own innocent body. Although He was completely innocent of all sin, He suffered the most horrible, disgraceful punishment known.

Nicky Gumbel, writing on 'Why did Jesus die?', observed that most leaders who have influenced nations or even changed the world, are remembered for the impact of their lives. Jesus, who more than any other person changed the face of the world history, is remembered not so much for his life but for his death. Why is there such a concentration on the death of Jesus?

Jesus suffered and died on the cross to absord the wrath of God. (1 John 4:10) Since God is just, those who sin must be punished. (Romans 6:23; Ezekiel 18:4) The love of God therefore moved him to send His own son to absorb His wrath and bear the curse (propitiation of our sins) for all who trust him. (Galatians 3:13) It was the will of God to crush Jesus for the wages of our sins. God planned for Jesus' death (Isaiah 53:10) so Jesus' willingness to die was an act of submission and obedience to the will of God. No doubt Jesus' death on the cross was a fragrance offering and sacrifice to God. (Ephesians 5:2) For our sake God did the impossible by pouring out His wrath on His son. Jesus offered Himself without blemish to God for us because we have sinned and have fallen short of God's glory. His blood was the only perfect thing to please God due to His sinlessness. Jesus Christ became human (mortal to be able to die) so that through death He might destroy the devil (Hebrews 2:14).

Jesus is the mediator of the new covenant (Hebrews 9:15). His blood was the blood of the covenant, which was poured out for many (Mark 14:24). The blood of Jesus therefore purchased the power and the promises of the new covenant. The death of Jesus guarantees the inner change in humanity (the law written on their heart) and the forgiveness of our sins. When we were dead in our sins, God made us alive together with Christ. This spiritual life, writes John Piper, has enabled us to see and believe in the glory of Christ. The arrangement has secured our faithfulness. It has put the fear of God in us which makes us reluctant to turn away from God. (Jeremiah 32:40) We can persevere because Jesus still intercedes and advocates for us while God keeps us.

Think about this, 'the hardest thing God could do is 'to give up his only son Jesus Christ to suffer and die on the cross'. Comparatively, one of the easiest things God can do is to give us all things that pertain to life. (Romans 8:32) If God had done the hardest thing of forsaking His son, it is certain that He will supply our needs according to his riches in glory. God's total commitment to give us all things is more sure than the sacrifice of His son.

God will meet every real need. He will give us all things that are good for us. All things we really need in order to be conformed to the image of Jesus Christ. (Romans 8:29) All things we need in order to attain everlasting joy. Every need includes even the ability to rejoice in suffering and the grace when many felt needs do not get met. Our heavenly father will empower and strengthen us to do His will to attain eternal life.

Prayer
Maranta leuconeura, a member of the family marantaceae is a plant native to the New World tropics. It is commonly called prayer plant or praying hands because it has spreading leaves that turn upward toward evening. Turning upward toward God is prayer. It is conversing with God, our heavenly father. It is a divine-human conversation. Like all conversations, it is

an informal exchange of ideas. It involves both talking and listening. When you are 'chatting with God' you need to express yourself in the same kind of language you use when talking to your close friend. God, like all good fathers, delights in the natural and uninhibited approach of His children.

There is however more to prayer than conversing with God. Prayer means four things:

- Entreating spiritual power
- Transacting spiritual business
- Receiving spiritual secrets
- Developing spiritual love

Though prayer is calling to God in times of need for his provisions, blessings, power, protection, and intervention, we also enter into a partnership with Him. We take authority and command in Jesus' name. God then releases His power in the heavenlies. Through prayer we receive spiritual secrets. God reveals the deep and secret things. (Daniel 2:22) In prayer we also give thanks and rejoice over all God has done for us. We become grateful for whom He is. It is a close intimacy with God. Out of this intimacy, God supplies our needs. Prayer is not just the mouth, mind and head that talk. It is our life that prays. Life that springs forth from a heart hungry for God. Lack of spiritual hunger is the root cause of our powerless prayer.

Why should I pray?

Prayer is God's greatest desire. It is no wonder that God's prime complain against man was made when Adam failed to fellowship with him in the Garden of Eden 'Where are you?' (Genesis 4:8-11) Genesis 4:8-11, illustrates a pathetic and sad scene. 'Here comes the Lord for an evening walk and a cozy chat. But Adam and Eve who had 'become wise', hid themselves from God. What had been a perfect, shameless fellowship had turned into a dreadful fear of God.' God who desires fellowship did not destroy both of them immediately. He called out and interacted with them. What would have been the result if Adam and Eve had entered the throne of grace and sought forgiveness. The Bible says 'Come now, and let us reason together, says the Lord. Though your sins are like scarlet, they shall be as white as snow; though they are red like crimson, they shall be like wool. If you are willing and obedient, you shall eat the good of the land ...' (Isaiah 1: 18-20)

God is forever prepared to pardon sins if we repent and turn to Him. We may contrast Adam's response to that of David when he sinned against God. 'And David said to Nathan, "I have sinned against the Lord," And Nathan said to David, "The Lord also has put away your sin; you shall not die"'. (2 Samuel 12:13) David did not attempt to rationalise his sin or to make an excuse for himself. He was pardoned. He loves us and always willing even to fix our sins when we come to Him. We have a standing invitation to come boldly to God's throne. (Hebrew 4:16)

Prayer is our privilege. It is an opportunity to have a heart-to-heart with our most gracious God. God hears our prayers. Many prayers may seem to have gone unanswered but maybe that is because the way we seek God in prayer is wrong. God is not far off if we seek him in the right way. (Acts 17:27) God wants us to pray to Him and not to someone else, a human being. All prayer should be directed to the Creator of the Universe. (Hebrews 11:6; Matthew 6:9; Matthew 4:19)

Owing to our imperfection, God has provided 'helpers' to speak for us in heaven and on earth. Jesus is our High Priest who speaks for us in heaven (1 John 2:1) and the Holy Spirit guides us in prayer. (Romans 8:26) The Holy Spirit will lead us in prayer and teach us all we need to know if we only yield to him. God requires us to recognise Jesus' position and purpose and to offer all our prayers in His name. (John 14:6; John 16:23)

If we want our prayers to please God, we must be sincere in trying to live life in harmony with God. (1 Peter 3:12) God's eyes are open to righteousness. He who turns his ear away from hearing God, even his prayer is something detestable. (Proverbs 28:9; Proverbs 15:29; 1 John 3:21-22)

Our requests must be in harmony with God's will. (James 4:3) Pray in faith. (James 1:5) It is good to have privacy in personal prayer; (Matthew 6:6) jargon and big words are unnecessary, what matters is what is in our heart. (2 Chronicle 16:9) Pray from the heart with humility. (James 4:6) Appreciate the privilege of prayer and pray without ceasing, it is not something of the last resort. Approach God regularly with expressions of thanksgiving and praise, as well as, with petitions and requests.

The benefits of prayer

Praying mantis gets its name from the way it holds its forelegs in front of its head, as though it were praying. It is very fierce and uses its legs to catch insects. The front leg works like a penknife. When an insect comes within its reach, these two parts, which are called tibia and the femur, are opened out and the insect is seized with lightning speed, held between the two rows of teeth and slowly eaten. Prayer is not something done because we have to, or to please God. It is for our own good. (Phil 4:6; Matthew 11:28; 1 Peter 5:7) Prayer is a golden opportunity, a privilege for Christians. God has committed himself to act in answer to prayer. (Luke 11:9-10) He is willing to change His plans in response to prayer. (Genesis 18:20-32; Exodus 32:9-14; 2 Kings 20:1-6) Through prayer, God's kingdom can be more fully established on earth. (Matthew 6:10) Through prayer, we get to know God and so we build relationship with Him. Through prayer we can change circumstances and situations to be in line with God's will and heart. (Ezekiel 22:30) Through prayer we can bless others and save them. (2 Kings 4:8-17; 1 Samuel 12:19)

Prayer brings glory to God (John 14:13). It binds demonic activities, the enemy of our welfare. It releases captives. Prayer weakens the grip and hold of Satan's power on the souls of men. When the grip is weakened, the captives will walk away in freedom. Prayer is our weapon to dislodge Satan and his hordes of demons. Without prayer, we are unarmed and weaponless for the battle. Prayer contributes to our spiritual growth. We get spiritual nourishment from our day-to-day prayer. Prayer releases forgiveness, strength, peace, guidance and the Holy Spirit into our lives. It releases faith. Whenever we pray, we are declaring that we do not have confidence or trust in the arm of flesh and thereby arrange for God's direct intervention. It makes us into people of authority and anointing. It creates and gives birth to new dimension in life. Prayer avails much. Prayer has great effects. It makes us accomplish much in life.

We all reach times in our lives when no human help is available or when the help humans offer is not sufficient for our needs. Then it is to God alone that we must turn. However, if we love God and appreciate the privilege of prayer, we certainly will not wait for such occasions to speak to Him. Instead we will approach Him regularly and frequently. Prayer shows recognition of our complete dependence on God for everything. It draws us close to fellow believers. It brings upon us the peace of our loving heavenly father. It promotes the flow of the Holy Spirit in our lives. It helps us to be confident about the future. It is a gift from God and one that we should appreciate and use. It brings marvellous benefits.

Who of you by worrying can add a single hour to his life? (Matthew 6:27) The word of Jesus about worry demonstrates that it is unnecessary, useless, blind and self-harming. We all have worries at work, in our homes, at school but it is always advisable to turn them into prayers. Carrying our worries, stresses and daily struggles by ourselves shows that we have not trusted God fully with our lives. In truth the only way to worry less is to pray more. In view of this, whenever we start to worry, we must stop and pray. (Philippians 4:6)

Prayer is the key to our spiritual growth
All animals and plants have to breathe in order to stay alive. Prayer is the Christian vital breath and native air. It is the heart of devotional life in that spiritual growth is determined to a large degree by how effective we are in prayer. Prayer must be indispensable and integral part of our life if we want to advance in our walk with God. Play games with your prayer life and you

shall fall prey to spiritual weakness, indolence, lethargy, sluggishness, fear, insecurities, and worries, writes S. Hughes. Nobody has neglected prayer and grown spiritually. Pray without ceasing and you will be a great person of faith – a person of great exploits, a person of authority and anointing. Tremendous power is made available through prayer.

Satan is afraid of praying Christians

After World War I, the League of Nations tried to secure global agreement on disarmament at a conference which opened in 1932 and ended in 1934. They achieved nothing. The invention and spread of atomic and hydrogen bombs brought new and greater threats to the future of mankind. Various talks and treaties – Strategic Arms Limitation Talks (SALT) between the USA and USSR in 1969; SALT II Treaty of 1979; International Peace talks (INTL) of 1987; the Strategic Arms Reduction Talks (START) of 1980 – were all efforts to reduce or ban nuclear missiles.

Prayer is a missile and the foundation of spiritual warfare. According to Dag Heward-Mills, those who discover this truth will have a great and fruitful Christian life. Spiritual warfare is born and maintained in an atmosphere devoid of prevailing prayer; when the warrior starts praying warfare will cease.

Prayer does two things to Satan: it binds demonic activities in our lives and releases people from his captivity. We must bind his activity, which causes backsliding, immorality, sin, poverty, depression, oppression, accusation, slander and disloyalty. Prayer weakens the grip and hold of Satan's power over people, when it is weakened, they walk away in freedom. Prayer is our missile to dislodge Satan and his hordes of demons. Without prayer, we are unarmed for battle.

Moreover, prayer releases faith, for whenever we pray, we are declaring that we do not have confidence in the arm of flesh and thereby arrange for God's direction. Prayer makes us into people of authority and anointing.

Satan is afraid of praying Christians because prayer works and it brings the power of God into our lives; we can resist the devil and defeat his purposes when we understand the authority we have in Christ. (James 4:7; 1 Peter 5:8-9) Satan will not catch us off guard when we watch and pray. (Matthew 26:41)

Prayer brings about God's will and thwarts Satan's. It brings us into a deeper relationship with God, which is the very thing Satan does not want. Satan, therefore, tries hard to wipe out our prayer life or at least to make it ineffective. The tools he uses include: distraction, temptation, ungodly thought, condemnation and encouragement of our doubts, fears and despair.

Deadly sins in prayer

Poisons injure the body and sometimes cause death. There are many sorts of poisons and terrible accidents are often caused by carelessness with them; some because people do not realise that a substance is poisonous. Some drugs for example are useful when taken in small quantities but are poisonous in large quantities. Like poisons, there are some deadly sins in prayer that should be avoided if we want to catch God's ears.

Praying to attract the attention of others indicates that our audience is not with God, for prayer is supposed to be a private business with Him. Although there is a place for public prayer, and there is nothing intrinsically wrong with high-sounding phrases, religious jargon and pious clichés in prayer, it is not, however, a sufficient condition for effective and powerful prayer in itself. Prayer should be simple, direct, concise and down to earth – a straight-to-the-point conversation with God. S. Hughes says that prayer should be free of showmanship for there is no reward offered by God to those who use prayer to show off their ability with words. It is wrong to pray with an improper motive. Many a time, the motive of praying determines the method of praying; why one prays determines how one prays. There may be nothing wrong with the words used in prayer but the motive may be suspect. There is nothing wrong in learning from others, watching and listening to how they pray, their zeal, actions and words. Nevertheless, we must not allow their experiences to overawe us. In prayer, we are not obliged to follow a pattern of prayer used by others. Some people are introvert in prayer while others are more extroverted. The ministries of Elijah, Jesus Christ, Hanna, Moses, Jacob and David are the most famous examples of fervent prayer but it is interesting to note that each of these people had his or her own style and pattern. You may copy someone else's style and pattern if it suits your personality and temperament but find your own style and pattern of prayer and, most importantly, be yourself with God.

The Bible is a book of hope
Sinatra had lost all courage and was hopeless. She planned to commit suicide before she was introduced to Mavis. At first she was unwilling to listen, but with kind perseverance Mavis was able to interest her in the study of the Bible. Within few a months, she had an entirely different outlook – filled with hope.

The Bible when properly understood is really the book of hope. It was written for our instruction and encouragement, that through our endurance and the comfort from it, we might have hope. The author is called 'the God who gives hope'. (Romans 15:4,13) The knowledge of the Scriptures affects our attitude towards the present and the future. The more we know about what God has done in years past, the greater the confidence we have about what he will do in the days ahead. The Bible has set so much store by hope. Hope is referred 50 times in the New Testament and is listed together with faith and love as the most important things in life.

We cannot do without hope. It is a necessity not a luxury. Without it man is prone to turn to loose conduct and despair. The Bible gives strong hope because it's God's Word, one who cannot lie. (Titus 1:2; Joshua 21:45; 1 Kings 8:56) As we grieve and fear because of constant wars between nations, sicknesses and diseases, death, bringing untold hardship, we are inclined to be discouraged. The Bible comforts us with God who cares, (Isaiah 41:10; Isaiah 12:2,3; Psalm 50:15) the hope of a glorious future, a future peace, a new world order where there shall be no more sicknes, death, war and grief. (Revelation 21:4) The Bible is a book of hope. The only way we can strengthen our hope is to feed our spirit regularly on it. We should read it diligently to increase our trust that God's will is best for us.

Why do we need to know the Bible?

Newspapers interpret events behind the news, such as social trends and political developments. In addition, newspapers give useful information, such as stock market prices, weather reports, and television viewing schedules. It is also a popular source of reading for entertainment. God uses the Bible to speak to man and when we properly apply it to our lives we shall be able to live a victorious life.

It makes us WISE. (Psalm 119: 98 – 104) It gives us LIGHT, a lamp to our feet and a light to our path. (Psalm 119:105,130) It gives PEACE and STOPS US FROM STUMBLING. (Psalm 119:165) It BUILDS us up and GIVES US AN INHERITANCE. It enables FAITH. Faith comes by hearing, and what is heard comes by the preaching of Christ or the Word of God – the Bible. (Romans 10:17) It gives ENCOURAGEMENT and ENABLES HOPE. For whatever is written in the Bible – in the former days was written for our instructions, that by endurance and the encouragement from the Bible we might hold fast to and cherish hope. (Romans 15:4) It is useful for instruction, for reproof and conviction of sin, for correction of error and discipline in obedience, for training in righteousness, in conformity to God's will in thought, purpose and action, so that we may be complete and proficient, well fitted and thoroughly equipped for every good work. It is FOOD for our spirit. Man is a spirit, has a soul and lives in a body. The Spirit is the real person. That means that our bodies are just containers of the spirit. The Word of God and prayer build and develop the Spirit. The Bible is alive and full of power; it is sharper than any two-edged sword, PENETRATING TO THE DIVIDING LINE of the breath of life and spirit, and of joints and marrow, exposing, sifting, analysing and judging the very thoughts and purposes of the heart.(Hebrews 4:12) We are drowning in a sea of impurity. Everywhere we look we find temptation to lead impure lives. The only way we can stay pure in our filthy environment is by reading God's word for counselling and strength and doing what it says

The Holy Spirit

Power. Power play. Power player. Power move. Power lunch. Power point. Power source. Power shortage. Powerful. Powerless. You quake in anger because you lack it, or you strut your stuff because you have it. Whether you want, understand or even care about power, God has determined that the primary way he will relate to us is through the presence and power of His spirit. So, if we want an encounter with God, we have to come to terms with the Holy Spirit, writes Dr Doug Beacham.

Think about this, 'the disciples of Jesus Christ were very slow in getting very enthusiastic in their new-found faith. They didn't seem excited about the relationship with God, with understanding things of the spirit or with praying (Matthew 26:40-41). On the day of Pentecost, they were filled with the Holy Spirit, which transformed their lives. (Acts 2:4) Great big smiles, boldness, discernment and witness became their trait. They became well known lighthouse of the world, a magnetic personality. People were drawn to them and helped many others to believe and to be filled with the spirit in the way that they had been.' What was it that made such a difference to them? It was the experience of the Holy Spirit.

The spirit of God is referred to as the Holy Spirit. Sometimes the Holy Spirit is called 'the Spirit of (Jesus) Christ'. (Romans 8:9; Philippians 1:19; 1 Peter 1:11) 1 Peter 4:14 refers to the Holy Spirit as the 'Spirit of glory and of God'. There are times in the Bible when the Holy Spirit is simply called 'the Spirit'. (Genesis 6:3; Numbers 11:17; John 3:34) The phrase 'the Spirit of the Lord' is found throughout the Bible (twenty-eight times).

In answering the question 'Who is the Holy Spirit?' we can safely say he is God. As God he is everywhere and ever present. He is all-knowing and all-powerful. Like Jesus Christ, the Holy Spirit has existed and continues to exist eternally as God. (Hebrews 9:14) He is the wisdom of God. (Proverbs 8:22-31) He was the active presence of the Spirit moving over the unformed and dark earth, bringing order out of chaos. It is valuable to observe, writes Dr Doug Beacham, that the presence of the Spirit at creation is connected to the voice of God who spoke into existence things that did not exist. (Romans 4:17; Revelation 4:11) The presence of the Holy Spirit in our lives means that God, who created the world, also created us, and He wants to speak to us to bring order out of our chaos (troubles).

The delight of the Holy Spirit

The stories of the men and women on United and American Airlines flights on 11 September 2001 are compelling. Those people knew they had but minutes to live. In their final minutes they called their families with messages of love and faith. We cannot understand Jesus' teachings about the Holy Spirit in John 14-16 unless we remember that everything he said and did was in the span of a few brief hours on the Thursday night that He was betrayed. Think about this, 'I will never leave you nor forsake you' 'It is expedient for you that I go away. For if I go not away, the Holy Spirit will not come. But if I depart I will send Him to you'. (John 16:7)

The Holy Spirit is the believer's helper. He is our comforter, counsellor, advocator, intercessor and guide. The single greatest key to eternal success in any Christian's endeavour is allowing the full work of the Holy Spirit in and through us. The Holy Spirit works hand in hand in the transformation of the Christian. As the Christian desires and in active and expectant faith works towards his maturity, the Holy Spirit then exercises His prerogative of revealing and reproducing Christ-likeness in him in ever increasing splendour. It is the desire of the Holy Spirit that Christians attain abundant life – peace, joy, happiness and well-being promised by Jesus. He desires to make us overcome the world and through him God will do all that is in His heart to do for His children. The Holy Spirit wants to share His strength, power, wisdom and information with us.

Minister of Religion

Sheep were some of the first animals to be domesticated. They can live in poor pasture and survive extremes of climate. Nevertheless all sheep need special care at lambing time, in the late winter or early spring. They are affected by many parasites and diseases. Blowflies, maggots, ticks, lice and mites live in their wool and in their skins. They are also plagued by creatures living inside them such as worms and liver flukes. They can get worms by feeding for long in the same land, and liver flukes from stagnant water. They are also prone to foot rot from standing too long on wet grounds.

Jesus said that He would build His church (Matthew 16:18) and He has chosen to do this by giving gifts of men as leaders to the church, who will shepherd his flock from predators, parasites and extreme weather. (Ephesians 4: 11-13) They shall equip or prepare the Christian for service in the kingdom of God; to cause the Christian to be built up – to maturity and to unite fellow Christians in faith. The Shepherd needs to be able to bring the Christian – those in his care – to a place where Christians are responsible, caring and supportive of one another; calm, consistent, committed and joyful; continually steadfast in the Word of God; whole and complete in Christ; growing up into Christ in every way, being joined and held together in harmony where each person knows their place and gift, where they are no longer childish, spoon-fed and self-willed, stuck or stagnant in their spiritual life; tossed back and forth by waves of mood or emotion, lacking assurance and stability and blown here and there by every wind of teaching.

God expects us to hear the Word of God through the leaders of the church and take it seriously and personally (Romans 10:15-17; 1 Thessalonians 2:13); to submit to their authority and be obedient; appreciate and give them due respect and recognition (1 Thessalonians 5:12-13) and to be loyal and committed to them. When we submit to them, we are protected from the enemy, because the shepherd will be a spiritual covering for us. (Hebrew 13:7, 17)

How long can we live?

Adam died at the age of 930 years and Noah 950 years. Recent long-lived people reach around 118–120 years. Pierre Joubert was 118 years, Jeanne Loiuse Celment was 122 years (1875-1997), Sara Knauis was 118 years (1880-1998). With the improvement in medicine, sanitation and healthcare, it is assumed that modern people can live longer than 150 years with strength, vigour and accomplishment. Scientifically, regardless of how many years we might live, our physical body remains very young. Nature takes us apart and put us back together everyday. We replace the cells lining every time and moment. Based on the design of our physical bodies it is not obvious why aging should occur. We are wonderfully made for eternity.

Why eternal life?

Life everlasting is a natural human desire because God has put eternity into man's mind. (Ecclesiastes 3:11) Nevertheless, we are helpless in the face of death. In truth it was God's purpose that we enjoy everlasting life. It is God's gift to us. (John 3:16; Titus 1:2) It was our disobedience, when Adam and Eve sinned against God, that we lost the right to everlasting life. (Genesis 2:17) We were thrown out of the Garden of Eden, away from the fruit of the Tree of Life, else we might eat and might have the privilege of living forever. We became defective, imperfect and our bodies became programmed for death. (Romans 6:23) This purpose of God for man's eternity has not changed. (Psalm 37:29; Matthew 5:5) To carry out His original plan He has given us Jesus Christ as a ransom, a gift to redeem us from death. He is the way to everlasting life. (John 14:6; John 3:16) There is life beyond the grave, after biological death, and our life on earth is only a preparation for our life that will never end. Today a man, tomorrow none. But death is not the end of all who choose life through Jesus Christ

Getting the best from God

On whom do you rely? God or man?

People who believe in God rely on him and diligently seek to know and apply His wisdom in their lives (Psalm 118:8-9); they talk to him in prayer regularly. (Colossians 4:2) Our devotion to prayer is an expression of our faith that God answers our prayers and His wisdom is indispensable part of our decisions. We tend to rely on His wisdom and seek to please Him with obedience to His directives. If we truly believed in God, we would care enough to investigate what the Bible says He is. We would read, study and meditate on the word of God.

We always put our confidence in something or somebody. Pilots put confidence in their planes; children in their parents. If we are willing to trust a plane or car to get us to our destination, those who trust in God are willing to trust Him to guide them to their purpose in life and eternal destination. Who do you trust? Man or God? How futile it is to trust anything or anyone more than God. Think about this, 'Man's extremity is God's opportunity and it is better to take refuge in the Lord than to trust in man'. (Psalm 118:8)

- Have faith in the mysterious works and ways of God.
- Obey the Word of God.
- God created us to know Him and to live for Him. One does not know a living thing untill he knows not merely its past history, but how it is likely to react and behave under specific

circumstances. God has a lot of cover up, and does not show everybody all that is about Him. If He takes us into His confidence, and tells us frankly what is in His mind on matters of common concern, and if He goes on to invite us to join Him in particular undertakings that He has planned, and makes ourselves permanently available for this kind of collaboration whenever He needs us, then it will make a world of difference.

- Besides, we will not have a close relationship with God unless we have fellowship with Him regularly. We must spend time each day meeting with Him and learning to communicate with Him. In this way we will be building relationships with the source of life and truth. The greatest we can offer God is the gift of our precious time. Time is more precious than any possession. The essence of relationship is not what we do for each other, or what material objects we give each other, but how much ourselves we give. 'Giving our time to God matters to him.'

- Do not forget the doings of God. King David never ever forget anything God had done for him. Listen to him, 'Bless God, O my soul, and do not forget all his doings. (Psalm 103:2) Appreciation is the key that opens up many avenues for expressing our thanks to God, writes a tabloid. We must not forget little kindnesses and not remember small faults. How quicly people forget! How success – prosperity and luxury – makes us ingrates. How quickly do we allow satisfaction to blind us, to forget God. Prosperity more than poverty, can dull our spiritual vision because it tends to make us self-sufficient and eager to acquire still more of everything – except God. We desire to worship money, movie stars, politicians, rulers even ourselves or something illusive. God's word is discarded. We must turn to God. We must never ever forget anything He has done for us. (Psalm 103:1-6) To help ourselves not to forget God, we must review, keep reading, keep listening to God's word. We must keep on glorifying God by being His witnesses. We must get acquainted with what He wants us to do and then do it. We must always remember that gratitude is the least of virtues, but ingratitude is the worst of vices. Gratitude preserves old friendships and procures new.

- Finally, we must receive Jesus as the developer of our faith (Hebrews 12:2) the same way we received Him as saviour. Jesus came to the earth because He knew our separation from God. He came to restore to man what had been lost, and allowed us to have a relationship with God again. He understood the problem and He Himself became mankind's answer. He is the Way, the Truth and the Life. He is able to lead us into eternity because He came out of eternity. 'He came out of the everywhere into here in order to lead us from here to the everywhere'. The Son of God became the Son of Man in order that the sons of men might become sons of God. Jesus Christ had become the foundation and centre of man's hope. He is the answer to life and God's provision for humanity's victory, peace, joy, health, wealth, wisdom, redemption and salvation. To whom else can we go in the troubled world to be assured of hope? There is no one but Jesus...' For God so loved the world that He gave His one and only Son, that whoever believes in Him shall not perish but have eternal life.' (John 3:16) Accept Jesus Christ as your Lord and Saviour, get close to God in prayer and keep His Words and life everlasting will be yours in Jesus' name. Amen.

18

Is money evil?

Bankrupt tourists are flocking to up-market Tunbridge Wells and Greenhithe in Kent after paying up to £7,000 to a British-based insolvency agency offering to find them a place to live and a job. Once secured with work and proof of residency, they can file for bankruptcy after 12 months, and a year later they can look forward to heading home debt free. The recession has seen a rise in bankruptcy tourism from around 20,000 per annum to 100,000.

I am content in whatever circumstance I am in. I know this very well. My key to life is simple. 'I am content with every situation'. I know what it is to be in need and what it is to have plenty. I have learnt the secret of being content in any and every situation, whether well fed or hungry. Nevertheless, I have learnt over and over again throughout my life that money is not inherently evil. 'Money is the answer for every thing.' (Ecclesiastes 10:19) But I prefer saying money is the answer to most things. It is used as a measure of value, as a means of storing wealth and for buying and selling goods. Money can be used for righteous purposes to carry out God's work: caring for the poor and needy and community development. When money is used for righteous purposes its rewards amount to, among other things, 'laying up treasure in Heaven'. (Matthew 6:19-21) It is the worship of money that is evil.

Love for money was referred to as mammon by Jesus. Mammon is an Aramaic word, which, essentially, means 'riches', suggesting greed, covetousness and selfishness around money. People under the influence of 'riches' trust in it more than God and believe that money can bring them happiness and fulfilment. Mammon attempts to usurp God and people; it breeds pride and leads to all sorts of sin: marriage and relationship breakdowns and robbery for example. It is impossible to 'serve' mammon and God at the same time, warned Jesus. Whoever loves money never has money enough. (Ecclesiastes 5:10) Those who love money and seek it excessively never find the happiness it promises. Wealth attracts scroungers and thieves, causes sleeplessness and fear, and ultimately ends in loss because it must be left behind. (Mark 10:23-25; Luke 12:16-21)

No matter how much you earn, if you try to create happiness by accumulating wealth, you will never have enough. Whatever your financial situation, do not depend on money to make you happy. Use what you have for good causes instead. It is God's blessings that make a person rich and add no sorrow. (Proverbs 10:22) Recognising God's blessings will profoundly impact on your perception of money and the way you live your life.

Financial difficulty

In truth poverty is a disease. When poverty comes in at the door, love flies out of the window. It is my prayer that God will meet all your needs according to his glorious riches (Philippians 4:19) Amen.

A recent study showed that more than half of Britons are struggling to make ends meet on their current income. About 58 per cent of people said they did not have enough money to meet their household bills comfortably. Reasons behind financial difficulties ranged from having wage increases capped, the decrease in property values, to losing all material wealth through bad investments or business decisions. A lack of the former money-making opportunities, the old established ways having changed, have resulted in less income for many and resulted in not having enough money to pay for essentials. There is only one thing that is certain at such times. Lack of money creates fear and uncertainty; it is extremely worrying and frightening. You feel unable to do anything; you are so preoccupied that even to think straight is difficult. Concentration is lacking and your performance at work suffers or you find it impossible to focus on looking for work. You feel withdrawn and panicked as you imagine all the worst scenarios unfolding. The temptation to pretend the whole thing isn't happening, to blank it out by eating, drinking and sleeping too much, or watching television excessively, is very real. You focus on the problem rather than the solution and pull yourself and others down by amplifying your worries.

Please, take comfort from the fact that the situation you find yourself in is not necessarily your fault. Stop blaming yourself or others for what has happened. The old rules of life simply don't apply anymore. Believe that there is a way to resolve the situation and that better circumstances and situations lie ahead. Thoughts that nothing is working should be banished from your mind; move on and look at helpful, practical steps to handle the strain of the situation.

Taking positive action will diminish the fear, so communicate with those to whom you owe money; small regular payments may be acceptable to them. Work out how you can create more money, however small the amounts. Believe in God and His Word, this will help you to see things in a more positive light. The righteous man may have many troubles but the Lord delivers him from them all. (Psalm 34:19)

Making money our master rather than our slave is wrong. I read of this article in the Watch Tower magazine that Money Sickness Syndrome, a term coined by Dr Roger Henderson, a mental-health researcher in the United Kingdom, afflicts a large percentage of the world. Money Sickness Syndrome is the physical and psychological symptoms experienced by people who are stressed with money worries. The symptoms include shortness of breath, headaches, nausea, skin rashes, lacking appetite, unjustified anger, nervousness and negative thinking.

In good times and bad times, many people, both rich and poor, are relatively free of anxieties about money and material possessions. People who are highly motivated by money and controlled by money are led to stress and neuroticism. Contrarily, those who budget their money carefully tend to have an internal locus of control and positive feelings towards themselves. They have lower stress and lower strain and are the masters and not slaves of money.

Money may be your master if you avoid discussing finances because of the anxiety it causes; when it is often the subject of your family squabbles; when you spend compulsively; when you worry constantly about bills; when you are not sure how much you earn or spend or own; when your bills are often bigger than you expect; when you often pay your bills late; when you are able to make only the minimum payment on credit card bills; when you pay bills with money earmarked for other things; when you take on extra work just to pay the bills; or have taken out new loans to pay off old ones, or use savings to pay routine bills, or find it impossible to get to the end of the month without running out of money; when you feel pressure to accumulate large sums of money and suffer physical and/or psychological symptoms resulting from money-related stress.

I believe that measure is treasure. Measure is medicine. We should all learn the virtue of moderation. Well stated, we must learn how to manage money wisely. Think about this parable of Jesus Christ in Luke 14:28 'Will he not first sit down and estimate the cost to see if he has enough money to complete it'. Britain's debt will hit £1,260 billion next year, while unemployment will creep towards ten per cent, a top think tank claims. The Organisation for Economic Co-operation and Development report predicts that debts will reach 90 per cent of the £1,400 billion Gross Domestic Product. It is advisable not to develop a fondness for money and devote ourselves to the accumulation of riches. (I Timothy 6:10) However, money is not evil, and when managed properly, it can be a useful tool. It solves a lot of problems. (Ecclesiastes 10:19)

- Make saving a priority. As soon as you get paid, deposit the amount you wish to save in a bank to overcome the temptation to spend this fund.
- A good budget gives you a sense of where your money goes. It can help you to reach your financial goals. It is the only practical way to monitor, control or reduce your spending.
- Carefully consider your future needs and plan towards them. The plans of the diligent surely make for advantage. (Proverbs 21:5)
- Invest in yourself acquiring new skills and taking care of your physical and emotional health. Make learning a lifelong habit. (Proverbs 3:21; Ecclesiastes 10:10)
- Keep money in its place. In truth, people who care more about people than they do about money are happier. Greed throws us off balance. A tabloid counsels that cultivating contentment prevents us from developing the love of money and all the problems that come along with it.

Proper management does not come naturally to most people, it takes a strong character. Since diligence is a great teacher, makes an expert workman and brings luck, it should be our indispensable mark in handling money.

The purpose of having plenty!

There is a secret known and practised by many wealthy people. Many of the rich people and nations of our world have discovered the purpose of having plenty and they have been blessed as a result. God blesses us with abundance, so that out of it, we could share with others in need. (2 Corinthians 9:8-9; Genesis 12:2) He wants to bless us with plenty but we miss the opportunity to give an enormous gift that would have brought us hundredfold in return. (Proverbs 11:24; Mark 10:29-30)

God rejoices over our wealth and abundance. (Deuteronomy 8:18; Psalm 31:19; Romans 2:4) He has promised to give his people 'the power to make wealth that he may confirm his covenant which he swore to your fathers ...' (Deuteronomy 8:18) He does not oppose wealth, what He opposes is 'putting our trust in wealth instead of him'. (Psalm 37:3; 1Timothy 6:17) It is trust rather than money that is at issue; the condition of the heart rather than the conditions of finances with which God is concerned, because it determines what we treasure the most. (Luke 12:34) Money is not evil or good in itself, writes Vikki Burke. It is neutral and intended to be used as a tool in the hands of those who trust the Lord to do His work. Many a time there has been the danger of misplaced trust, becoming proud and forgetting the Lord. (Deuteronomy 8:12-14) A person is a fool to store up earthly wealth without a rich relationship with God. (Luke 12:21) If our wealth increases, it must not be the centre of our life rather we must be God's distribution centre to bless humanity. Nabal inherited the land that once belonged to Caleb but could not inherit his character. Nabal was wealthy but rude, snarling, boorish, surly and coarse. He was blinded by his wealth and accustomed to the prestige, influence and power that wealth brings. Out of the kindness of David's heart, he protected Nabal's sheep from thieves and predators. When the day came to show gratitude to David, he repaid him with insults and humiliation. Giving is a sweet smelling odour to God. The gifts we give others are a fragrant offering, an acceptable sacrifice, pleasing to God.' (Philippians 4:18)

Perfumes became popular in Europe in the 16th century, although only rich people could afford them. The main reason people used perfume was to hide their smell, for in those days baths were rare. Queen Elizabeth I was thought to be exceptionally clean because she had a bath every three months. Giving is 'a sweet smelling odour to God'. (Philippians 4:18) It is an aroma, a perfume, a smell especially a pleasant one. It is a sacrifice acceptable and well pleasing to God. It is important to God because, in Paul's words, it tests the sincerity of our love for God and others. How we handle material wealth is a barometer of our spiritual health. (Matthew 6:19-21)

We should not give primarily to get. Nevertheless, giving does lead to abundance. Cheerful givers experience God's love in a special way. (2 Corinthians 9:7) They enjoy the spiritual blessing of participating in a rich harvest of righteousness. (2 Corinthians 9:10) Think about this: 'In a joyful and magnificent devotion to the Lord, Noah sacrificed animals and birds he had preserved on the ark. The sacrifice was acceptable and pleasing to God. He thereby vowed never to repeat the awful devastation of the earth that the flood caused, although he knew that the conditions of humankind had not changed.' (Genesis 8:20-21) Abraham offered God a sacrifice and received a guaranteed promise back by a covenant from God on the same day. (Genesis 15:7-21) The desire of King David to build God a house won him great favour from God, to preserve his throne forever. (1 Kings 11:9-13) By faith the widow of Zarephath gave far beyond her means to Elijah, and her faith-giving did not deplete her natural resources. (1 Kings 17:16) Dorcas was restored to life from death because of her good works and charitable deeds. (Acts 9:36-43) God gives great rewards. He loves to reward us when we diligently seek His presence, His will and His ways. He rewards good work, stewardship and generosity. (Hebrews 11:6; Hebrews 6:10) No doubt, Abraham, Jacob, David, the widow of Zarephath and Dorcas walked in a blessed life.

Remember always that it is cheap enough to say, 'God help you'.

Blessings are better than riches

Experience is the best teacher. I have also experienced this. There is a blessing better than riches. The blessing of loving God. The Lord watches over all who love Him; He hears their cry and saves them'. (Psalm 145:20) Think about these sayings: 'That never ends ill which begins in God's name'; 'God, parents and our masters can never be requited'; 'He who serves God, serves a good man.'

Bob Gordon expresses that 'God loves those who draw close to Him, and loving Him brings many blessings':

- He is faithful, keeping his covenant of love to a thousand generations (Deuteronomy 7:9; Exodus 20:6);
- His love will follow all those who love Him (Psalm 23:6);
- He watches over them (Psalm 145:20);
- He loves them (Proverbs 8:17);
- We know that in all things God works for the good of those who love Him, who have been called according to His purpose (Romans 8:28);
- No eye has seen, no ear has heard, no mind has conceived what God has prepared for those who love Him (1 Corinthians 2:9);

- God lives in them (1 John 4:16);
- Neither death nor life, neither height nor depth, nor anything else in creation will be able to separate us from the love of God that is in Christ Jesus our Lord (Romans 8:37-39).

'The blessings of the Lord brings wealth, and add no trouble to it.' (Proverbs 10:22) Prior to the recent financial crises – the credit crunch – writes a tabloid 'a new generation of young adults in the United States were displaying a propensity for splurging on luxury items. However their spending power was not bringing them happiness rather their affluence was one of the principal causes of alcoholism, depression and suicide.' A study revealed that despite abundance and wealth, 'fewer than one in three Americans claimed to be very happy'. Awake magazine reported that Andrew Carnegie, a pioneer of the steel industry and one of the richest men in the world, was interviewed and said: 'I am not to be envied. How can my wealth help me? I am sixty years old, and I cannot digest my food. I would give all my millions if I could have youth and health'. Carnegie told the interviewer that he is convinced that there are blessings greater than material riches.

Daniel Gilbert, a professor at Harvard University, notes that mental health experts 'have spent decades studying the relation between wealth and happiness and they generally concluded that wealth increases human happiness when it lifts people out of abject poverty into the middle class. Once above the poverty line increases in income have surprisingly little relation to personal happiness. Money doesn't necessarily have any connection with happiness.' 'Maybe with unhappiness', commented the oil magnate and multi-millionaire, Paul Getty. This is an assertion the Bible trumpets. (Ecclesiastes 2:9-11; Ecclesiastes 5:12-13; Proverbs 10:22; Proverbs 30:8-9)

We can find true and lasting happiness when we satisfy our spiritual needs; if we put God first we will find that every aspect of our life becomes richer and more rewarding. The struggle to get material wealth and keep it allows time for little else. Living by God's principles opens up so many blessings: happier marriage, peace of mind and a good conscience.

We show our love for God when we are grateful for who He is, when we give thanks and rejoice over all He has done for us; when we desire to know Him better; when we live a life that pleases Him and become obedient to His Word and commands; when we express our love to Him through music, dance and prayer; by telling Him we love Him; when we become His witness, salt and light of the world, loving our neighbour and even our enemies. Always remember that, 'if God is for us, who can be against us?' (Romans 8:31) God himself is the help of the helpless.

19

THE SCANDAL

Women are necessary evils

University sex scandal! Women do better; men earn more. The Higher Education Policy report revealed that women are trouncing men at Britain's universities. More women attend university (49 per cent of women against 38 per cent of men), and they are less likely to drop out once there and they get better marks. They also do better in tougher courses, such as medicine and law. Men are more likely to go on the dole after university but male graduates who do find job are paid more.

Who is who? Is it male or female? Are they in competition or complementary? In truth, from the beginning, men and women were equal beneficiaries both of His divine image and of earthly rule. (Genesis 1:26-28) The word 'man' in Genesis 1:26-28, doesn't mean 'male' as opposed to 'female'. It means 'humanity', a generic term for the human race. It means from the beginning there was a single genus – one kind – but two types of human beings: male and female. They differ biologically, physically and psychologically but complement one another. Each has an inherent sexuality and that sexuality differs; each has a sexual organ that is made to fit together in a way that God our heavenly Father designed.

When the Bible says 'It is not good for man to be alone, I will make a helper suitable for Him', (Genesis 2:18) it implies that the creation of man was not complete until God made woman. Without female companionship and a partner, man could not fully realise his humanity. There is no doubt that in many cultures, women have been habitually despised and demeaned by men – treated as mere playthings and as brainless simpletons incapable of engaging in rational discussion. Their gifts are unappreciated, their personality smothered, their freedom curtailed, and their service in some areas exploited, and in some cases refused.

The status and service of women have been rapidly changing, especially in the West, thanks to the feminist movement and Acts such as the Sex Disqualification Act of 1919.

All human beings, male and female, are equal beneficiaries of the divine image and earthly rule. (Genesis 1:27) Neither sex is more than its creator, or more responsible for the earth than the other. John Stott was right when he commented that because men and women are equal, there can be no question of the inferiority of either to the other. And because they are of equal dignity, men and women must respect, love, serve and not despise one another. Because they complement one another, men and women must recognise their differences and try not to eliminate or usurp one another's distinctiveness.

We must permit women to accept or gratify their basic need to grow and fulfil their potential as human beings. Any culture that forbids women to pursue their own career or earn their living must be reviewed. The factor that should influence our different and appropriate roles in society must be the distinctive qualities of our sexuality, psychological as well as physiological. God wants us all – male and female alike to be fulfilled not frustrated, and the world to be enriched by the services of everyone. Anyone with talent and ability should be given the opportunity to succeed. It is my prayer that as the cage door has been opened, the canary will fly out. Women everywhere, get excited at growing to your potential.

The reality is that the ideal woman is an excellent wife and mother. She is versatile – a manufacturer, importer, manager, estate agent, farmer, seamstress, upholsterer and merchant. (Proverbs 31:10-31) Such outstanding abilities, position her high in the family status. No wonder God envisaged that 'I will make a helper suitable for Him.' (Genesis 2:18) Without female companionship and a partner, man cannot fully realise his humanity. God has equipped women for a task. She is man's helper. She was made to help man in every aspect of his life. She is a comforter, counsellor, advocator, intercessor and guide. It is the desire of the ideal woman that man attains life abundant – peace, joy, happiness. She is ready to share her strength, power, wisdom and information with him – to 'share the same pillow'. She is man's greatest partner in life. In situations where the going is tough, she takes hold of the situation with him, adding her strength to his – the synergy effect. She will take hold together with him. She is not doing it for him but with him. She does it in him, with him, with his participation or involvement. No matter our belief system, 'man and woman were created perfect for each other. She is the bone of man's bones and the flesh of man's flesh ...' (Genesis 2:23)

Releasing the powers of women

According to Lee Grady, damnable lies have been used for centuries to keep women in bondage, fear, depression and in their God-given gifts, destiny, purpose and authority. The following statements are shocking: 'Women are not equipped to assume leadership roles in the church. Women must not teach or preach to men in a church setting. A woman should view her husband as the "priest of the home". Women are more easily deceived than men. Women can't be fulfilled or spiritually effective without a husband and children. Women shouldn't work outside the home. Women must obediently submit to their husbands in all situations.'

What lies are these to tell women they are not good enough and that they will never measure up to men. In essence, this low view of women is rooted in a misconception that the first female, Eve, was created by God as an inferior creature with deficient physical strength, less astute mental capacities, and limited spiritual giftedness, and because of her weakness was meant to live in a state of subordination to Adam. It is the idea that because Eve was deceived by the serpent, she must forever be punished for her disobedience by living in the shadow of her superior male counterparts. Eve was not inferior to Adam. She was his 'help mate', a companion, a word that denotes intimacy and partnership. God said it was not good for the man to be alone, (Genesis 2:18) acknowledging that Adam was in an inferior condition without a mate. Eve's subordination to man did not occur with her making, it was the consequence of her sin.

Kathrn Kuhlman (church minister), Catherine Booth (wife of the founder of the Salvation Army), Joyce Meyer (Christian author) and

Michael Marnu

Margaret Thatcher (UK Prime Minister 1979–1990) and many more women like them, have impacted on the lives of millions globally, and we look back to their achievements with gratitude. According to Lee Grady, we are all created with a unique destiny that we are all able to fulfil regardless of gender. Women are not inferior to men. Eve's subordination to Adam did not occur with her creation but as a consequence of her sin, and God handed down punishment to the man, the woman and the serpent. When God said woman 'Your husband will rule over you' (Genesis 3:16) He did not want things to stay that way. He provided a saviour, Jesus Christ, who carried the curse for us. (Genesis 3:15, Galatians 4:4) Jesus challenged the cultural bias against women that was pervasive in Israel at the time. Women were viewed as evil, ignorant and repulsively immoral. They were not allowed to enter parts of the temple and were segregated from men in the synagogue. Jesus lifted women from the agony of degradation and servitude to the joy of fellowship and service. (Luke 8:2-3)

Every man is the architect of his own fortune. Women are the 'sons' of their own works. Think about some of the negative sayings about women: 'No war without a woman'; 'there is no devil as bad as she-devil'; 'women are the snares of Satan, the devil's, net'; 'no mischief but a woman is at the bottom of it'; 'they are like a weathercock and as wavering as the wind; hate and love at extremes'; 'they naturally deceive weep and spin'; 'they may be saints in church, angels in the street and devils at home'; 'they have long hairs and short brains'; 'they need but look on her apron-string to find an excuse'; 'their sword is their tongue, and they do not let it rust'; 'they will say anything'.

Women's first line of defence is to wake up and reposition. Men and women have distinctive qualities, both psychological and physiological, a fact that should influence our different and appropriate roles in society. The cage door has been opened, let the canary fly out. Women everywhere, get excited and grow to your potential.

The secret of manhood

I observed that in many homes, trust and respect for men are on the decline. The call for respect from their wives is on a more serious note than ever. I firmly believe that respect isn't something you demand. It is rather reciprocal. What goes round comes around, writes Rich DeVos. Think about this: 'A good name is more desirable than great riches'; (Proverbs 22:1) a good name is 'better than fine perfume'. (Ecclesiastes 7:1) According to Dr Ed Cole, a good name is an essential qualification of a good man, for it commands respect and trust. The good name is the difference between a man and a male, for being a male is by birth but being a man is by choice. To be a man one must set up a standard of character.

The key to a good name is three-fold involving promise-keeping, responsibility and wisdom. Man has been created in God's image, and because God's creativity is in His Word, this is our image too. 'Life and death lies in the power of our tongue.' There is power in our word too, and we should, therefore, take words very seriously. As God's Word is important to Him so shall our word be to us. Do you keep your word? Are you full of truth or lies? How do your wife, friends and society assess you regarding your word? This is a test of your manhood. The word of a man should be his bond; your word should be an expression of the nature and measure your character. Are your words full of profane, swollen, foolish talk? Trust is extended at the level of truth and half a truth is a whole lie, so without truth there is no trust, no confidence and no respect. Lack of trust is the cause of many broken relationships, for no one can submit to what he does not respect. Let your name be as good as your word. Your word should be the source of people's faith in you; a rule of conduct in your own life. Remember the sayings, 'he loses his thanks that makes promises and delays' and 'to him that breaks his trust, let trust be broken'.

Realise also that it is said a long tongue is a sign of a short hand, that is, to offer much, is a kind of denial. I will leave you with two further sayings on the subject: 'he that promises much means nothing'; 'eggs and oaths are easily broken'. Do not be most eager to make promises you cannot or will not keep.

I would like to conclude this chapter by throwing a lucid light on singleness and the joy of sex.

Being single

A gunman killed three women and wounded nine others when he opened fire on a gym class. George said nothing before spraying the studio with 52 bullets from two weapons, and then he killed himself. He kept a web page describing years of rejection by women. It listed the date of his death and his status as 'never married'.

Singleness, like childhood, is experienced by all of us; at one time or another we all lead a single life. It may be for a short period only, or it may be for a long time. Clearly there are certain individuals that God calls to a life of singleness in order to fulfil a specific purpose that He has asked of them. (Matthew 19: 10-22) There are those called to a life of celibacy, and who are at peace with having no life partner, but there are others that feel pressurised by society for being single and wish they were not.

Some single people despise themselves, but Colin Dye believes those who are single should redeem these years and not demean themselves. Like couples, single people can enjoy every season of their lives and should not dismiss what God has ordained for a blessing.

Learn to use your single years positively, not drifting through life believing that there are roses beyond the horizon and that all fun, enjoyment and satisfaction starts from the moment of marriage. There is something singles can do better than couples: to be the light or the salt of society, now, before tomorrow when their circumstances may change. Let your light shine out and glorify God with your singleness.

When single it is better to abstain from the extremely potent force of sexual relationships, which the enemy can capitalise on to defile your singleness. Protect your sexuality while single; see it as a dynamic potent force that God insists we keep safe until within the heart of marriage.

The joy of sex

Sex is God's idea, a gift from God, a wonderful, precious, pure and holy thing that is to be used as a means of glorifying Him in the context of marriage, writes Colin Dye. From the very beginning of creation, God made male and female, two types of human beings. (Genesis 2:26-27) Men and women differ biologically, physically and psychologically and yet they complement each other. Each has an inherent sexuality that differs, and sexual organs that are made to fit together. Sexuality is designed for reproduction: God commanded us to be fruitful, multiply and replenish, implying that it was God's command that we enjoy sex. It is unfortunate that in contemporary society th real joy of sex has been crushed and trampled upon. God gave us sex for both reproduction and enjoyment according to specific criteria centred on a secure and loving relationship. The purpose of sex is blessing, intimacy, joy, pleasure and multiplication.

It is God's plan that sexual relationships are completely mutual; a gift and a blessing to married partners. (1 Corinthians 7:3) Married couples should not deprive one another of intimacy, but, nevertheless, there are times when married couples should focus on concentrated prayer and fasting to perhaps see a specific breakthrough in prayer.

Sexual sin

Many sexually transmitted diseases (STDs: syphilis, gonorrhoea, genital herpes and AIDS caused by the HIV virus) are spread by sexual contact. According to the media, Britain is now the HIV king of Europe, but it seems that the sexual revolution and the ensuing no-strings attached sex craze isn't as problem-free as some think. Some good old monogamous relationships might help the situation, and according to one tabloid newspaper, even those who have protected sex with multiple partners are still liable to contract and spread STDs.

Sex is a sacred act that should not be practised outside marriage. Outside marriage it becomes a destructive force driven by desire. Sexual esire outside marriage poisons souls and wrecks lives. Every other sin committed by man is outside the body, but sexual immorality sins against his body. (1 Corinthians 6:15-20) Be mindful at all times of the sanctity of sex. Recognise its potential and consequences over any desire for enjoyment or gain.

20

MAKING YOUR MARRIAGE SUCCESSFUL

When a couple could not agree on a name for their newborn girl they decided to reach for the nearest mobile phone and called a text-message question and answer service. Two minutes later the couple received a name they could both agree on. At the beginning they wondered what people would think about how they came up with the name but now they think it's just a nice story. Although it is a trivial, nice story, it can nonetheless set fire to a forest. Marriage is for life, yet the number of couples that divorce continues to rise. In 1987 in Britain out of 398,000 marriages there were 165,000 divorces. Many marriages which began with tender love and rich expectations now lie in ruins.

There are three main purposes for which marriage is ordained:

- The procreation of children together, bringing them up within the love and discipline of the family;
- To support, cherish and stimulate each other to fulfil each their destiny both in prosperity and adversity;
- The reciprocal commitment of self-giving love which finds its natural expression in sexual union, or becoming 'one flesh'.

John Stott has observed that the loving discipline of family life has become all the more necessary because of the waywardness of children; mutual support because of sorrows of a broken world; and sexual union because of the temptations of immorality. Marriage is a moral and spiritual commitment which should be honoured. (Matthew 19:6; Malachi 2:17) Divorce contradicts and frustrates the purposes of marriage, bringing both husband and wife acute pains of alienation, disillusion, recrimination and guilt, which precipitates in any children of the marriage a crisis of bewilderment, insecurity and often anger. Marital breakdown is always a tragedy. At the crux of any matrimonial offence that could put the marriage asunder, John Stott's fervent prayer resounds: 'we must always remember the covenant we made with our spouse in the days of our youth, and make it an everlasting covenant, to bring forgiveness and penitence.'

The secrets of successful marriage

Marriage is for life, yet the number of divorces continues to rise. Many marriages which began with tender love and rich expectations now lie in ruins. At the crux of marital conflict that could put a marriage asunder, Dr Bill and Bea Basansky's philosophy of successful marriage is worth considering.

The secret to a good and happy marriage is not so much finding the right person, as being the right person. Marriage provides a fertile ground for success or conflict. The idea of winning a marital conflict is an illusion. One's victory invariably becomes a loss for both. By sharing space and time, married couples limit one another's freedom in many ways everyday. How well the marriage works depends on a great degree of how well the couple learns to handle conflict arising from these limitations. Husbands and wives must approach their disagreements constructively by seeking to resolve rather than to win them. Watch out for the clues: 'win/lose tactics which do not resolve but fan marital conflicts; the use of extreme or irrational tactics to gain your point; willingness to hurt your spouse to win; use of emotional equivalents of street-brawl tactics, 'See, I told you it wouldn't work. I was right all along."

Marriage is a cooperative enterprise and not a competitive one. The goal is to reach a solution both of you can live with, a compromise that will make life together more pleasant rather than to settle which of you is wrong. Learn the art of effective and honest compromise where both partners are satisfied. It may not be ideal but a compromise that works is better than a brilliant solution that one partner is likely to sabotage. Avoid letting mild disagreements become full-scale battles. Difference demands coordination and communication not division and divorce. Do not expect too much from your marriage. Give it adequate time or energy to become established.

Dr Bill and Bea Basansky believe that every marriage needs security to grow and strive. Security means that we are fully committed to the truth and make a decision to be open to correction. It is assurance that someone is committed to love and values us for a lifetime. It is a constant awareness that whatever difficulties we face, we will work to solve our problems together. Security is built into relations each time:

- We speak the truth
- Go out of our way to encourage our spouse
- Listen without lecturing
- Give them a gentle hug.

Security is threatened when:

- We lie
- We do not keep a check on our tone or voice
- We are harsh instead of being soft.

Divorce contradicts and frustrates the purposes of marriage. It brings to both husband and wife the acute pains of alienation, disillusion, recrimination and guilt, and precipitates in any children of the marriage a crisis of bewilderment, insecurity and, often, anger. Marital breakdown is always a tragedy. God does not intend faithfulness in marriage to be boring, lifeless, pleasure-less and dull. He hates divorce. (Malachi 2:16) He wants us to rejoice in the wife of our youth. (Proverbs 5:18)

Dr Bill and Bea Basansky recommend four ingredients for a lasting marital relationship:

- Develop unconditional security, a lifetime commitment to care for your partner;
- Establish meaningful communication, daily sharing, feeling, needs, hopes, and dreams and be a good listener when the other person is sharing,
- Schedule romantic experiences. Set your schedule to include intimate times together or the pressure of life may set your schedule for you;

- Take time to touch. Eight to ten loving, intimate touches a day keeps the marriage counsellor away.

Do you know your partner?

I have also learned this over and over again during marriage counselling sessions. Obviously, we marry because we love each other and want to spend the rest of our lives together, yet the dream of a happy marriage often proves to be a 'dream'. We are so wrapped up in personal interest that often our partner, as far as their thinking is concerned, is a stranger to us. How well do you know your wife? Do you know what your wife was looking for from a husband?

Do you know your wife?

A woman wants someone to love her for what she is, someone to care for her, honour her and cherish her. She wants someone who will listen to her and take her seriously; someone to talk to about her feelings over issues and problems, about everything. She looks forward to a husband who will be a friend, a soul mate who will encourage her and help her in achieving her potential. The word of a man should be his bond. Our words are an expression of our nature. She desires a man who keeps his word: honest, open and faithful. Trust is extended to the level of truth, for remember that 'half truth is a whole lie'. If there is no trust, there is no confidence and no respect, for a woman cannot submit to what she does not respect. She wants a man she can share romantic times with, someone who is already romantic or willing to learn how to be, rather than a man who is in a relationship for 'easy' sex. A man can be the king of his house if he respects and understands the woman's opinions and feelings. Although a woman's place is said to be in the home, she longs for a man who will help her care for and teach the children. Man may be the head of the household, but a woman only respects a man who will lead the family, take the initiative in decision making and set a Godly example. 'If you make your wife an ass, she will make you an ox.'

Do you know your husband?

She admitted that her husband was 'no saint', insisting he 'loved' Britain, saying 'He is my husband, my hero. We have been married for nine years now. We have seen each other through some tough times, perhaps great times and we'll be together for all times. He's messy. He is noisy. He gets up at a terrible hour. But I know he wakes up every morning and goes to bed every evening thinking about things that matter.'

Marriage is a divine institution. It was established by God as a permanent bond so that we might be mutually helpful to each other. A good wife makes a good husband, and the best way for the wife to be the keystone of the house is to know more about the man she married and what he most looks for in a wife.

It seems there are three things men want from their wives: love, support and respect. Marriage is the tomb of love. He wants a woman who loves him for who he is; a woman who will support and encourage him when the going is tough. Honour shows the man and he desires mutual respect and honour in spite of circumstances. A man also wants someone to share his interests, secrets and vision and wants someone to understand his needs, concerns and challenges. He wants someone who will listen and not crow. Man is not looking for a master but someone to acknowledge his leadership within the home, someone with whom he feels comfortable. Life has mixed blessings, and it is for this reason that man is at home with someone who is loyal and will be a special friend throughout the highs and lows of life; someone he can rely on and trust. Marriage is God's gift. Couples were created perfect for each other. Among other things, marriage was instituted so that two become one flesh in the intimacy and commitment of sexual union that is reserved for marriage. Hence the man wants someone with whom he is sexually fulfilled. As we desire to spend the rest of our lives together happily in marriage we must always remember that an obedient wife commands her husband.

Dealing 'for better for worse' promise debt

At the crux of marital conflict my fervent prayer is that we always remember: marriage is for better or for worse. In the UK it is required by law that in marriage words of declaration and contract are said in the presence of an authorised person and two witnesses. One of the declarations is to affirm that the couples will love, comfort and honour one another through all the joys and sorrows of life, and be faithful to one another for as long as both shall live. One cure for marital breakdown is acceptance. Acceptance can transform relationships, as one psychologist expresses, 'No one has the power to reform another person, but by liking the other person as they are, you give them the power to change themself'. No wonder Jesus Christ 'had a way with people' while the good and righteous Pharisees never changed the conduct of any sinners. Take Hitler, a most ruthless man that set himself against the world, surrounded himself with a small group of admirers and took them with him everywhere he went.

As individuals we are hungry to be accepted as we are. We want to be able to relax, be ourselves and be accepted as we are – in sickness and in health. A moaning, nagging, complaining or scolding partner brings us to our knees; a critical, fault-finding type of person that sees where others fall short is never going to be an ideal partner. The more we set up rigid personal standards of how we think other people ought to act, we drive them away. People can never at all times do everything we do and like everything we like. Love sees no faults. Remember always that 'Do not be a bully if you want your partner to accept you, it is a good start to accept him or her. A deaf husband and a blind wife are always a happy couple. It is a sad house where the hen crows louder than the cock. He who marries might be sorry; he who does not will be sorry; the married man has many cares, the unmarried one many more; a man without a wife is but half a man and a cheerful wife is a joy of life'.

21

THE FUTURE GENERATION

The revolt of youth has become the talk of the day. Adults are pointing fingers. The crimes of violence in which youth indulge are without a cause; these are not ordinary social ailments. A tabloid recently asserted that today's youthful errors are either inclined towards violence, or they rebel against restriction so that they can engage in their sensual desires, enjoying the excitement of the moment. The youth are in their own world with certain beliefs, attitudes and convictions about life and society. Their lifestyle is one of live-for-the-moment.

'A bad workman always blames his tool.' 'A bad shearer never had a good sickle.' Where did it all start? 'He who spares the rod hates his son, but he who loves him is careful to discipline him.' (Proverbs 13:24) The greatest responsibility given to parents by God is the nurture and guidance of children. Lack of discipline puts parents' love in question because it shows a lack of interest in the development of their child's character. Disciplining children averts disaster, for without correction, children grow up with no clear understanding of the difference between right and wrong and have little direction in life.

In many instances, parents are to blame because the young act on what they learn at home. With our rebellious attitudes, shattered home discipline, lack of cohesion, unhappy families, rebellious spouses; wives rebelling against husbands and husbands failing to love their wives; less priority in spiritual things and parents failing to bring up their children, society is lost: a sheep without a shepherd, the blind leading the blind. 'But how can the cat help it, if the maid be a fool?' Let the buck stop here! We have all rebelled against God and our children are rebelling against the elders.

Raising a family is like growing a garden
In 1884, churchman Benjamin Waugh wandered south London's slums and was appalled by the harsh lives many children suffered. He was so moved by the sight of abused youngsters that he set up what has become one of today's most recognised charities – the National Society for the Prevention of Cruelty to Children (NSPCC). Its creation, 125 years ago was a bold move – a

family's privacy and right to raise its offspring as it saw fit was holy. Not everything has changed so dramatically, however, 'we still have cases of dreadful cruelty, such as Baby P' comments the NSPCC's executive director.

Many delinquents come from problem families where relationships within the family are excessively difficult. There may be violence or alcohol involved and the parents themselves may be criminals. More than 90 per cent of delinquents had unhappy home lives and felt discontented with their life circumstances. Many of them had parents with whom they did not get along or who were inconsistent in their patterns of discipline or punishment.

Children are our heritage. The fruit of the womb is a reward. Like arrows in the hand of a warrior, so are the children of parents. The quality of a garden is the pride of the gardener; likewise, children should be wanted, nurtured and loved. Love shared among family members is essential to a family's survival, for without love, a home becomes a house where people merely eat to leave as quickly as possible. Parents misdirect their love when they show more concern for family projects than for family members, when they put a job before their family or overcompensate and spoil their children.

The power of effective training lies not in what a parent may say and teach, but in what they do. Sometimes children feel and declare that their parents are over-protective; they worry too much, they don't listen, they are hypocritical, and they profess to be something they are not. We cannot teach children ideals we fail to live up to ourselves. When we live what we teach, we are able to teach others to live. Love that draws us closer is more than what laws demand.

Lessons learnt in childhood will last a lifetime

'Train a child in the way he should go, and when he is old he will not depart from it.' The verb 'to train' means 'to dedicate, to develop or equip', and the 'way' generally refers to living correctly in God's sight. Parents are not only obligated to care, nourish and support their children, but also to set the child aside for special tutoring, stimulate the child to do good through encouragement, guidance and discipline. Training and development should be part and parcel of every childhood; otherwise raw, God-given talents could become wasted and abused. Parents must help their children identify their seed of destiny, their future career, and guide them and nourish their ambition and talent. Whether a child learns to follow correct living will, in part, depend on his own choices, but lessons driven home at the crucial stage of childhood will not go away. Hence the need for good parenting, discipline and guidance

The child is operating in a world opposed to restrictions and discipline. There is a mighty tide of lawlessness running through society. Many people seem to believe that individuals should be allowed to do what is right in his or her eyes. Now, more than ever, loving discipline must be administered to children. A child should never be left to feel despised and unwanted by their parents; never let discipline become harsh and hard. It must be exercised for the right reasons and in the right way or it will do more harm than good. Remember that raising a child takes great wisdom. Remember always that youth and white paper take any impression

Begin to understand youth and learn to meet their needs

I firmly believe that the starting point of building a good foundation for our youth is to begin to understand them and learn to meet their needs. Forget the fact that the headlines focus on a country riddled with teenage knife culture and gun crime. Young people are more likely to die by their own hand than be killed in a violent attack. A recent study reported in the medical journal, Lancet, says that road accidents are the single biggest killer of young people in Britain, with violence only coming in at number five. (London Metro 11 September 2009). No matter how we see the youth of today, they are full of ideas and vision. They have been created in the image of God and are responsible people. They too have a conscience to discern between alternatives, and freedom to choose between alternatives. They will be accountable for their actions. With youth, compulsion is never the key; persuasion by argument is far more effective. Begin to understand the youth and learn to meet their needs. This is the key to transforming our streets.

Should adults impose their views on the youth?

The imposition of adults' views on youth is an area where most youth and many adults disagree. To young people, elders are out of step with their generation. While certainly adults should come to terms with the young and their ideals, I wonder to what extent? There are three possible responses regarding adults' influence over youth: imposition; laissez– faire and persuasion by argument.

Most adults long to see a society that reflects the virtues of life, so the desire to achieve this by force is tempting. It has been observed, however, that any attempt to impose belief and behaviour is unproductive, for no one can force people to practise what they do not want to practise. To force our convictions and standards on youth, therefore, is unrealistic, foolish and nostalgic.

On the other side of the coin is the laissez-faire – the let-people-do-as-they-please – stance. A principle of non-interference by parents, it appears to be more about a mood of apathy and indifference; leaving the young alone to mind their own business, where far from imposing our views, we do not even commend them for the things they do right. The laissez-faire attitude is not a trouble-free one. How is it possible to be tolerant of a lifestyle known to be evil or erroneous? 'He who spared the rod spoils the child', wrote wise King Solomon.

Persuasion implies that while we should get involved in building the character of youth we must treat their conscience with respect. Their conscience may be weak or strong; a weak conscience (over-scrupulous and full of qualms) needs to be strengthened, while the deceptive conscience needs to be enlightened. There should be no bullying of conscience, however, only in the most extreme circumstances should a person be induced to act against his or her conscience, writes John Stott. Conscience is to be educated not violated.

In all our dealings with youth we must remember they are versatile, young and full of ideas. They are the leaders of tomorrow, our pride and future.

Danielle Strickland's thoughts are worth considering as to how we can step beyond preconceptions about marginalised young people in their communities. She suggests five steps to transforming our streets:

- Find them where they are.
- Pray for them.
- Talk to them.

- Be friends with them and go into partnership with other local youth groups.
- It would take a whole community of committed people to make the transformation happen.

A tabloid recently commented that it seems we are so wrapped up in personal interest that our children are becoming strangers to us. We are shocked if they get into trouble or run off but we cannot see where we have failed them. Children are the future and many sayings make the point of the wealth invested in them: 'children are a poor man's riches'; 'happy is he that is happy in his children'; 'invariably youth never casts for peril and if they knew what age would crave, they would both get and save'; Nevertheless, we should not let our children sleep on bones. Train them up properly in the way they should go.

The key to transforming our streets

An Agape 'Right from Wrong' survey found that 11–18 year-olds who have abandoned any notion of absolute truth were twice as likely to get drunk, and three times as likely to get into pornography and gambling. About 75 per cent of them also thought that lying was necessary.

The greatest responsibility that God gives parents is to nurture and guide their children. Lack of discipline puts a parent's love in question because it shows a lack of interest in the development of the child's character. Disciplining children averts disaster. Without correction, children grow up with no clear understanding of right from wrong and see little direction to their life.

Pray for children and ask God to offer a strategy. See children with the eyes of Jesus and talk to them, asking 'What do you need?' The strategy should come out of their needs. Be friends with them; one good relationship is enough to start with. Establishing a real relationship with children that creates trust can take a while and requires that we stay on their level. Building such relationships will bear fruit; those on the fringe will come into the fold.

Too often today children are seen as a liability rather than an asset. In truth, they are 'a heritage from the Lord, a reward, our future and pride. We will not be put to shame when we contend with our enemies at the gate.' (Psalm 127:5) Those who view children as a distraction or nuisance may realise in future that 'a child's service is little, yet he is no little fool that despises it.' See our youth as an opportunity to shape the future. Remember always that soft wax will take any impression. Diligent youth makes easy age.

Don't look for answers through drugs: they don't help

Nevertheless, it is advisable for young people to keep away from the spate of knife and gun attacks, the gang culture and drugs.

More than 11,000 children in England were treated last year (2008) for addiction to drink or drugs. The total included 6,075 under-16s who were hooked on cannabis. Of those, 102 were under 12. The figures, from the National Treatment Agency for Substance Misuse, show 11,294 under-16s were receiving help for addiction. Of those, 4005 – 57 of whom were under 12 – were treated for alcoholism. A further 232 were being treated for cocaine misuse, 36 for crack, 165 for ecstasy and 93 – including ten under the age of 12 – for heroin addiction. There were also 22 under-12s who were treated for solvent abuse.

The quest for meaning and purpose of life through drugs is a sham and futile because attempting to solve one's problems through drug abuse often leads to a greater problems. Addicts develop a tolerance to drugs, which means they have to take increasing amounts of the same drug to satisfy their physical needs and to avoid withdrawal symptoms. When an addict is deprived of a drug, they experience agonising withdrawal symptoms, which can include severe pain, convulsions and vomiting. Most addicts can only buy the drugs they need through illegal sources. Drugs acquired illegally are often diluted or incorrectly mixed and can caused sickness when taken. They are also expensive and addicts may have to turn to crime to be able to afford them. An addict who has an expensive habit will spend most of his money on drugs, leaving little left for food. People who inject themselves with drugs using hypodermic needles often suffer from infections and put themselves at high risk of contracting HIV/AIDS.

Drug abuse is not clever or glamorous, or an answer to life's problems. It is unhealthy. It is dangerous. It can lead to crime and prison, and it can kill. God is willing to help all who are trapped by addiction if they will humbly call upon him.

Above all, I wish no youth to say or even imagine 'had I known' because 'it is always at last'. I have learned this over and over again throughout my life. And it is very vivid at the time of my fragile age. If things were to be done twice, all would be wise. Life is half spent before we know what it is. Think about this, 'Too much liberty spoils all'.

The meaning of freedom
As S. Hudges observed even the most casual observer of life on this planet cannot help but notice that the desire for freedom is to be found in every human heart. Everyone wants freedom, but so few know how to get it. The popular notion of freedom is that the fewer

restrictions that are placed upon us, the freer we will be to develop our potential and be the kind of people we were meant to be. This is not the way to true freedom but rather it is the way to bondage. Seek freedom first and you will never find it, for freedom is a by-product of obedience. Those who put freedom first find that the only freedom they obtain is the freedom to get tied up with themselves and with others.

'Some people try to find freedom by doing what they like: others try to find freedom by doing what they ought.' Only those who take the latter way find true freedom. The former kind of freedom turns to futility, the latter to fertility.

S. Hudges counsels that although God has created us as free agents, we are not made primarily for freedom. We are made primarily for obedience. The first lie ever told was about human freedom. Satan said to Adam and Eve, 'If you do as you please you will be like God.' Adam and Eve did as they pleased and lost God's glory and goodness. They ruined their lives and futures.

At the centre of freedom is obedience to the right thing or to the right person. Your obedience to the wrong authority can land you in bondage. (James 1:25) A perfect law turns out to be perfect freedom. According to John Stott, 'freedom is not freedom from responsibility to God and others in order to live for ourselves, but freedom for ourselves in order to live for God and others.' The more we are caught up in Christ, the more freedom we shall experience and enjoy. It is freedom that Christ has set us free. In bondage to Christ we experience the greatest freedom the heart can never know.

Good foundation

'An idle youth, a needy age but a diligent youth makes easy age.' Youth today, adult tomorrow. No matter how you find yourself, remember that now is the beginning of your life. It is not the end of your life. It is the beginning of a great thing, a future glory and honour. Let today be a dawn of a new day, a stir of hope, a beginning of imaginative visions for the future. No matter how dark your situation seems, how insignificant or useless you feel, there is hope.

Everything must have a beginning. If the beginning is good, the end must be perfect. A good beginning makes for a good end. An ill beginning makes for an ill ending. Such a beginning and such an end well begun is half done. There is no good in building without a good foundation. When life is calm, our foundations don't seem to matter. But when crisis comes, our foundations are tested. Think about this, 'in a calm sea, every man is a pilot'. Be sure your life is built on the solid foundation so that you will bring joy to your parents' heart, then they can answer anyone who treats them with contempt (Proverbs 27:11) and that they will not be put to shame when they contend with their enemies in the gate. (Psalm 127:5)

I wish above all things that youth should use their time to lay a solid foundation for their lives. They are the future generation of leaders of tomorrow. Now is the time for their personal development and empowerment.

22

THE CONCLUSION OF THE MATTER

'Blessed is the woman who gave you birth and nursed you', (Luke 11:28) a woman in the crowd called out. Blessed rather are those who hear the word of God and obey it. (Luke 11:29) Jesus' response to the woman meant that a person's obedience to God is more important than his or her place in the family. The patient work of consistent obedience is even more important than the honour of hearing 'stuff'. Everything has an end: 'the end crowns the work' they say. 'All's well that ends well.'

At last, we have come to the end of the book. We have listened, learnt, meditated and prayed but 'if better were within, better would come out'. Singly or together I am sure we will make a positive difference. Each and every one should take the once-in-a lifetime initiative and make a simple heartfelt goal or commitment, keep it and record it for history. Eventually we will all do something. A vision without action is just a hallucination, writes Anderson Scott. Take time to deliberate, but when the time for action has arrived, stop thinking and go for it, writes Napoleon. God's glory is upon us because he wants us to operate in great fame and wealth. We are a part of the Abrahamic covenant in which God said 'I will make your name great and you shall be a blessing...'; (Genesis 12:2-3) a part of the Adamic covenant in which God, having made us in his own image, blessed us with usefulness and dominion; (Genesis 1:26-28) and a part of the New Covenant, which makes us heir to the heavenly dominion with Jesus. We must forcefully forge ahead without allowing anything to distract us from our purpose. We must develop a passion to do whatever it takes to succeed. A passion to be fruitful will drive us to learn basic skills we cannot do without. Empty your best into the present. Run life with excellence.

Journal

Observation: What have I learned?	
Relevance: How was it important to me?	
Decision and action: What I have decided to do.	
Notes	

'MY COLLECTION'

"If a seasoning has no flavour, it has no value". The world is never impressed with people who are unsuccessful, poor, powerless and weak. 'My Collections' aims at building the right foundation for Christian living. It is priceless and can be likened to precious jewellery that brings beauty and value to the user.

The Series
Spiritual Journey, the Milestone of Spiritual Life

The Christian life is a journey. It has a beginning and a destination. The book tells the milestones of this spiritual journey and how to make it to the end.

Time with God, Pain or Joy?
How can we afford God's primacy when we have many other urgent things that demand our time and attention? The book instructs how to make our time with God vibrant, stimulating and effective.

El Elyon, the Highest God
It introduces us to the nature, power, love and plans of God for His children and how His Children can get the best of His good plans for them.

Jesus Christ, the Bread of Life
Jesus is the answer to life and God's provision for humanity's victory, peace, joy, health,

wealth, wisdom redemption and salvation. The book teaches us how to appropriate Jesus' legacy in our lives

The Holy Spirit, Our Ideal Helper
The book throws a lucid light on the fact that the single greatest key to eternal success in any Christian endeavour is allowing the full work of the Holy Spirit in and through us and how he can make us overcome the world.

Satan, the Fallen Angel.
Recognise, Refuse & Resist Him
It is a contemporary approach to spiritual warfare. It shows us the cunning schemes of Satan and how to recognise, refuse and resist him.

Sign Post, Where to look when you need help
It gives us quick relief when we need help. It will help us empower ourselves by making the most of our God-given talents and opportunities which many of us don't take advantage of.

Reflections,365 Days of Wisdom, Strength & Guidance. A Daily Devotional
It contains 365 days of devotional strength, guidance and wisdom, offering penetrating insights on how we can achieve self-worth, success and fulfilment and make our lives productive.

Making Your Life a Success
Wisdom, Strength & Guidance for Life

Life may never get that bad for us, if we know what it is to live in a world of uncertainty and confusion. In this masterpiece, I have shared with you wisdom, guidance and strength which revolve around philosophies, beliefs, values and character traits that have proven to be the most sustaining and valuable in life.

Bibliography

Dr Anderson, C. Thomas, Becoming a Millionaire God's Way: Getting Money to You, Not From You, Faith Words, USA, 2006.

Beacham Jr, A. D., Light for the Journey, 2nd Edition, Lifespring Resource, Georgia, USA, 2000.

Beacham, Doug, Plugged into God's Power, Charisman House, Florida, 1979; revised in 1982 by Thomas Nelson.

Bilby, Ian, Hope, Explaining, Sovereign World, England, 1994.

Boteach, Shmuley, Dating Secrets of the Ten Commandments, Double Day, New York, 2000.

Bradfield, Phil and Potter-Longman, Steve, GCSE Biology, Pearson Education, 2002.

Calkins, Harold, Book of Uncommon Prayer, Autumn House, Lincolnshire, 2002.

Carnegie, Dale, Stop Worrying and Start Living, 1948.

Cerullo, Morris, God's Victorious Army Bible, Morris Cerullo World Evangelism, 1996.

Children's Encyclopaedia Britannica, Encyclopaedia Britannica, 4th Edition, 1988.

Cleghorn, Patricia, The Secrets of Self Esteem: A New Approach for Everyone, Element Books, 1996.

Draw Close to Jehovah, Watch Tower Bible and Tract Society of Pennyslavia, USA, 2002.

Fergusson, Rosiland, Penguin Dictionary of Proverbs, 2nd Edition, Penguin Group, 2007.

Fleming, Don, AMG Concise Bible Commentary, AMG, Tennessee, USA, 1988.

Giblin, Les, How to have Confidence and Power in Dealing with People, Hill Inc, Eaglewood Cliffs, New Jersey, 1956.

Godawa, Paul, The Art of Listening: Secrets Which Will Help You Gain Many Victories in Life, Wydawnictwo 'Woda Zycia' ul, Poland 2003.

Godawa, Paul, Understanding Life: Discover the Secrets of Life, Wydawnictwo 'Woda Zycia' ul, Poland, 2006.

Gordon, Vince, The Foundation of Christian Living, [n.d.]

Hagin, Kenneth, Bible Prayer Study Course, 14th edition, Kenneth Hagin Ministries, USA, 1987.

Hedges, Burke, You, Inc. Discover the CEO Within, INTI Publishing, Tampa Florida, 1996.

Hill, Napoleon, Napoleon Hill's Unlimited Success (52 Steps to Personal and Financial Reward), The Napoleon Hill Foundation, 1993.

Hill, Napoleon Think and Grow Rich, Random House, UK, 2003.

Isaiah's Prophecy, Volumes 1 and 2: Light for all Mankind, Watch Tower Bible and Tract Society of Pennyslavia, USA, 2001.

Maltz, Maxwell, Psycho Cybernatics, Pocket Books, NY, 1969.

Marshall, David, God's Little Book of Comfort, Autumn House, Lincolnshire, 2002.

Marshall, David, God's Little Book of Peace, Autumn House, Lincolnshire, 2003.

Marshall, David, God's Little Book of Promises, Autumn House, Lincolnshire, 2004.

Mesiti, Pat, Wake Up and Dream, Pat Mesiti Ministries, 1994.

New Encyclopaedia Britannica, Encyclopaedia Britannica, 15th Edition, 1994.

NIV/ Study Bible, Hodder and Stoughton, 1979.

Obeng Marnu, Michael, Thriving in Adversity (When everything says No in Life), Sovereign Venture, 2000.

Osward-Sanders, J., Spiritual Leadership, 2007.

Piper, John, The Passion of Jesus Christ, Crossway Books, 2004.

Prince, Derek, Blessing or Curse. You Can Choose, Chosen Books, a Division of Baker Publishing, 2nd edition, 2007.

Rashford-Hewitt, Andrew, 101 Proverbs for Life, Autumn House, Lincolnshire, 2008.

Stott, John, Issues facing Christians Today: New Perspectives on Social and Moral Dilemmas, Marshal Pickering, 1970.

Touch Points for Men, Tyndale House, 1966.

Turner, Colin, Born to Succeed: How to Release your Unlimited Potential, Element Books, 1994.

Wagner, C. Peter, Your Church Can Grow: Seven Vital Signs of a Healthy Church, Regal Books, USA, 1994.

Watch Tower, Watch Tower Bible and Tract Society of Pennyslavia, USA, (1960–2009).

What Does the Bible Really Teach? Watch Tower Bible and Tract Society of Pennyslavia, USA, 2005.

Williams, Gareth, Biology for You, National Curriculum Edition for GCSE, Stanley Thorne, 1996.